# *Remarkable* CHARLESTONIANS IN THE AMERICAN REVOLUTION

# *Remarkable* CHARLESTONIANS IN THE AMERICAN REVOLUTION

PETER McCANDLESS

*Forewords by Elizabeth Chew & William Baldwin*

Published by The History Press
An imprint of Arcadia Publishing
Charleston, SC
www.historypress.com



First published 2025

Manufactured in the United States

ISBN 9781467158732
Hardcover ISBN 9781540299956

Library of Congress Control Number: 2025941523

*The glorious fourth—again appears,*
*A day of days—and year of years,*
*The sum of sad disasters,*
*Where all the mighty gains we see,*
*With all their boasted liberty,*
*Is only change of masters.*
*—Hannah Griffitts, 1785*

# CONTENTS

# FOREWORDS

The commemoration of the 250th anniversary of the American Revolution, beginning in 2026, is providing welcome opportunities for public reckoning with this seismic event in world history. Fifty years on from the 1976 bicentennial, a time of patriotic fervor and freedom-branded consumerism, many Americans need a more nuanced understanding of what the Revolution accomplished and what it failed to do, who it freed from a tyrannical monarchy and who it left behind.

Academic historians have grappled with the successes and failures of the Revolution for well over fifty years, focusing on traditional military history and, beyond it, on the complex stories and fates of Loyalists, Native Americans, enslaved African Americans, LGBTQ+ Americans, non-elite Americans and women in all groups.

The South Carolina American Revolution Sestercentennial Commission was chartered by the South Carolina General Assembly in 2018. Through a statewide grant program and county-level 250th Committees, the Commission is working "to celebrate and promote our state's pivotal role in the fight for independence by educating, engaging, and inspiring both South Carolinians and visitors." Its grant program states that the "Commission also wants to intentionally seek out and give voice to previously disenfranchised groups; discovering the stories of SC's African Americans, Native Americans, and women and children who were essential to the birthing of a new nation."

The centrality of the Patriot victories at the Battles of Kings Mountain and Cowpens in upstate South Carolina to the turn of the war and Cornwallis's surrender in Yorktown nine months later is currently little known nationally. It is even little known in South Carolina, despite the state's long reputation for self-regard. Whether this relates to Northern influence on public memory of the Revolution following the Civil War or something else, the 250th affords a chance to shine a light on the complete story of South Carolina in the Revolution.

—Elizabeth V. Chew, PhD, Chief Executive Officer,
South Carolina Historical Society

*Remarkable Charlestonians in the American Revolution*, Professor Peter McCandless's contribution to the new literature, focuses on the wealthiest city in British North America in the unhealthiest of the thirteen colonies and the only one with a majority Black population. These conditions and others render Charleston a particularly interesting and resonant microcosm for examining the Revolution. In this excellent collection of short biographies, we see that the story of the American Revolution, like much history, is, in Professor McCandless's words, "unpleasant, messy and chaotic." Now is a good time for Americans to understand and acknowledge the complexity of our national origin story.

What follows is not just "another history of the American Revolution" but a study in personalities: both men and women, Patriots, Loyalists, enslaved and free men, driven by a complex intertwining of sympathies now comes our way. And we shouldn't be surprised to find both heroic and sinister effort on both sides, sides changing or death beyond the bounds of combat.

South Carolina's particular role in the conflict has sometimes been overlooked, especially following the Civil War—the war that began in Charleston. At least for some Southerners that appeared to be the case. Paul Revere and Bunker Hill loom large. But the first major Patriot victory was in that same southern harbor. There just over four hundred ragged men manned a small palmetto log fort on the harbor's Sullivan's Island and defeated eleven warships of the largest navy in the world. British cannon balls bounced off or were buried in the soft palmetto logs. British troops couldn't ford the deep swift breach at the island's north end. In Charleston, at least, June 28, 1776, has been celebrated as Palmetto Day or Carolina Day ever since, and always reference is made to brave Sergeant Jasper, who when the crescent-capped blue banner was shot down, exposing himself to fire, returned it to the wall attached to a cannon sponge staff.

"That they will stand by these colors as long as they wave in the air of liberty" wrote an officer's wife in presenting new colors. The pledge was made on behalf of Jasper and his fellow fighter and three years after the flags of the regiment were planted before the British lines in Savannah. Historian David Ramsey's account: "One by Lieutenant Bush who was immediately shot down. Lieutenant Hume, in the act of planting his, was also shot down and Lieutenant Gray in supporting them received a mortal wound. The brave Sergeant Jasper on seeing Lieutenant Hume fall, took up the colors and planted it. In doing so he received a wound which terminated in death; but on the retreat being ordered he brought the colors off with him. These were taken at the fall of Charlestown and are said to be now in the tower of London."

"History is often unpleasant, messy and chaotic. Historical myth is the opposite: neat, generally pleasing—at least to our prejudices—and comfortably black and white. The myths are 'alternative facts'—fake history," writes Peter McCandless in his conclusion. What you hold in your hand is "actual history." Of the people, by the people, complicated, gritty and vastly entertaining.

—William P. Baldwin, author of *The Hard to Catch Mercy* and many other works of prose and poetry about South Carolina

# ACKNOWLEDGEMENTS

The research underlying this book stretches back decades. Like all historians, I have benefited from the assistance of a large cast of archivists, librarians, fellow scholars and friends. To thank everyone individually here would take pages. But I must commend the staffs of the College of Charleston's Special Collections, the South Carolina Historical Society, the Waring Historical Library, the Charleston Library Society, the Charleston City Archive, the Caroliniana Library, the South Carolina Department of Archives and History, the UK National Archives at Kew, the National Archives of Scotland and the British Library. As for scholars whose work informed mine, their numbers are legion. Many of them can be found in the bibliography. I would like to extend special thanks to William P. Baldwin, Elizabeth Chew and Harlan Greene for their assistance. Chad Road, my editor at The History Press, was unfailingly helpful. Nalan gave me the necessary push to produce this book. Any mistakes remaining are totally mine.

# INTRODUCTION

## *Charleston's First Civil War*

Charleston, South Carolina, is famous as the place where the American Civil War began. Less well known is the significant role it played in an earlier civil war. For Charleston, the American War for Independence was more truly a civil war than the conflict of 1861–65. During the 1860s, Charlestonians were united in defense of their city. Dissenters from the decision to secede from the Union could be counted on one hand. During the War for Independence, in contrast, Charlestonians were bitterly divided. They denounced, exiled, fought and occasionally killed one another. Their divisions spread throughout South Carolina and became magnified, igniting some of the most violent and significant episodes of the War for Independence. This work examines the experiences of a spectrum of the city's inhabitants during this turbulent time. Its subjects were famous, obscure, rich, poor, Black, White, men, women. Some of them supported independence; others opposed it, tried to remain neutral or switched sides during the war. Collectively, their experiences highlight the reality of the revolutionary era. That reality was often grim. This is not a celebratory work. The public memory of the American Revolution is encrusted with layers of convenient forgetfulness, dubious facts, distorted legends and outright myths. This book seeks to portray the complexity of a chaotic, turbulent and fascinating time. The result, I hope, provides a nuanced sense of what it was like to live during the revolutionary years.

In 1775, Charlestown, as it was called until 1783, was the fourth-largest city in the thirteen colonies. With about twelve thousand inhabitants, it

*A View of Charles Town* by Pierre Charles Canot, 1768. *Library of Congress.*

trailed only Philadelphia, New York and Boston. It was a major port of the British Empire and the wealthiest city in the wealthiest of the thirteen colonies. In the decades just before the revolution, its wealth grew at a faster pace than ever before or since. In terms of income and material possessions, the merchant and planter elite were on a level with all but the richest British aristocrats. Educationally, South Carolina trailed less affluent colonies to the north. The elite never put much emphasis on or funding into education. A small number of charitable schools provided the most basic education for poor Whites. With few exceptions, Blacks received no education. Wealthy Whites made use of tutors and private schools to educate their children. The top ranks of the White elite sent their sons—but not their daughters—to Britain or the North for higher education. Unlike several colonies to the north, South Carolina did not establish an institution of higher education during the colonial period. Visitors marveled at the city's wealth but not its intellectual accomplishments. One remarked that the conversation of the merchants and planters was largely limited to horses and dogs or the prices of rice and indigo. Dr. Alexander Garden, who lived in Charleston for more than thirty years, lamented the lack of intellectual stimulation: "Here I am in Charlestown's blistering summer, stuck with the ox, the ass, and men as stupid as either," he wrote to a friend in England. The occupations of the "gentlemen planters," he claimed, were largely limited to "eating, drinking, lolling, smoking, and sleeping." They tended toward an arrogance common among men used to dominating others. Before the revolution, John Rutledge called the White inhabitants of the South Carolina backcountry "a pack of beggars."

The prosperity of Charleston on the eve of the revolution advertised itself through gleaming new buildings: the State House, St. Michael's Church, the Exchange and other public and private constructions. The buildings and the prosperity that financed them rested on a grim foundation, the labor of enslaved Africans. South Carolina was the only colony in British North America where Blacks outnumbered Whites. Blacks made up as much as 80 percent of the population in some Lowcountry parishes on the eve of the revolution. Another ghastly reality darkened the local scene. South Carolina was not only the wealthiest of the thirteen colonies but also the unhealthiest. While a small elite grew immensely rich, they often died young. Most inhabitants merely died young. Charleston and the

*Mr. Peter Manigault and His Friends* by George Roupell, 1760s. *Courtesy, Winterthur Museum.*

surrounding Lowcountry were notorious for deadly fevers. Malaria was a perennial danger, yellow fever a periodic one. Smallpox, dysentery and other diseases added to the grisly toll. "If you wish to die young, go to Carolina," was a common saying. Wealth and unhealth were intimately connected. Both stemmed in large part from the cultivation of rice with enslaved Africans. That Whites suffered terribly from disease in the Carolina Lowcountry has long been established. Infants and children died at an astonishing rate. In Christ Church Parish in the early eighteenth century, the parish register records that 86 percent of baptized children died before age twenty. The White death rate in early eighteenth-century Charleston was roughly twice that of the average parish in England or New England at the time. Between 1750 and 1779, planter Henry Ravenel and his wife had sixteen children. Only six survived past twenty-one. The six children of Elias and Mary Ball all died before age twenty.

The enslaved died fast as well. A lack of documentation and research long obscured that bleak reality, combined with the lasting power of a myth. The myth derives from the nineteenth-century proslavery argument that claimed that Blacks possessed immunities to the fevers that killed so many Whites. According to this convenient view, Providence had "designed" African constitutions for plantation labor. In contrast, some eighteenth-century observers remarked on the heavy mortality of the enslaved. Garden, who served as Charleston port physician in the 1750s, inspected newly arrived slave ships for signs of contagious disease. He was shocked by what he found. Many of the ships had lost as much as one-third to three-fourths of their "cargoes" during the voyage from West Africa. The ships on arrival were "so filthy and foul it is a wonder any escape with life." The hazards of the voyage were not the only ones. Many Africans died on the slave ships in harbor waiting to be sold. Their bodies were often thrown overboard into the Cooper River to save the expense of burial. In 1769, Governor Montagu condemned the practice as "inhuman and unchristian," as well as dangerous: "the noisome smell arising from their putrefaction may become dangerous to the health of the inhabitants." The practice continued until the slave trade became illegal in 1807. For Africans who survived long enough to be sold, high mortality was a fact of life, especially for those condemned to labor in the steamy, mosquito-infested rice fields. The whip and other instruments of torture added to the grisly toll. Garden treated many sick and injured slaves, of whom he wrote: "Masters often pay dear for their barbarity, by the loss of many valuable Negroes, and how can it well be otherwise—the poor *wretches* are obliged to labor so hard…and often overheat themselves, then exposing themselves to the *bad air*." The result was pneumonia and other respiratory disorders, "which soon rid them of cruel masters, or more cruel overseers, and end their *wretched* being."

Great wealth and high mortality help explain the Lowcountry elite's reputation for extravagant living. "Live fast, die young," could have been the region's motto. Charleston was a notorious party town for elite White men. Their wives and daughters had fewer options, though they did have the theater, music and the occasional winter ball, more entertainment than most colonial women. Planters, lawyers and merchants mingled in charitable organizations such as the South Carolina Society, the St. Andrews Society and the Fellowship Society. Considering the great wealth of the region, the money they raised for charity was not impressive. They were essentially social clubs that met at the city's taverns to indulge in drinking, gaming, horse racing and political chat. Men of all ranks, including artisans, shopkeepers, sailors, indentured servants, apprentices and urban slaves, flocked to numerous taverns and dram shops. Drunkenness among the "lower orders" was a cause of concern to the authorities, who tried to restrict it with little success. The city's brothels catered to other male activities. At "Ethiopian Balls," elegantly dressed women of color "entertained" young White men. Elite White men sometimes took "mulatto" mistresses, to the relief or disgust of their wives. The religiously devout denounced sexual promiscuity, drunkenness and gambling. Evangelical preachers like George Whitefield blamed the city's numerous epidemics, fires and hurricanes on such sins. But the devout only occasionally ruffled the feathers of the pleasure-seeking elite. One of Charleston's nicknames is the "Holy City," because of the number of places of worship located in its historic district. Their presence did not make it a puritanical place. Visitors, especially from New England, remarked unfavorably on Charlestonians' casual approach to morality and religion. They noted that the churches were rarely filled on Sunday, and men often chatted with one another during sermons and prayers.

The Church of England was the established church and the church of the establishment. The administrative unit of the colony was the Anglican parish. At the time of the revolution, Charleston was divided into two parishes. Their churches, St. Philip's and St. Michael's, were the only religious edifices that could call themselves "churches." The others, which catered to several "dissenting" Protestant sects, were called meetinghouses. The sects included Presbyterians, Independents or Congregationalists, Huguenots,

Baptists, Quakers and Lutherans. Methodists were relative newcomers, still shakily connected to but critical of an Anglican establishment they viewed as religiously "lukewarm." By eighteenth-century standards, Charleston was a relatively tolerant place for the Protestant sects and even Jews, who established their own meetinghouse. The tolerance derived partly from the need to keep the White population united in the face of the enslaved Black majority. Tolerance did not extend to one group of Christians: Roman Catholics. Their small and largely invisible community was technically illegal. They worshipped in secret.

The triumph of the revolution in South Carolina was nothing short of miraculous. At the beginning of the movement that led to independence, people who advocated resistance to the British government were a minority in the city and much more so in the wider colony. They called themselves Whigs or American Whigs and later, Patriots or Americans. They called their opponents Tories. As political names, Whig and Tory derived from British politics of the late seventeenth century. By the mid-eighteenth century, "Tory" had become shorthand for an authoritarian, royalist, intolerant person. Politically, Tories had been discredited and ceased to be significant. Ironically, American Whigs used the Tory label to discredit supporters of the British. For these reasons, I avoid using the term Tory except when it was used by the Whigs. I avoid the term Patriot as well, and not just because it is the title of Mel Gibson's revolutionary fantasy. People who became Loyalists were not markedly different from their opponents. They also considered themselves patriots. I use the term Whig a lot for colonists who supported active resistance to the British or Americans after they declared independence. Rebel, like Tory, is tendentious. I avoid it except when examining things from a Loyalist or British perspective.

Charleston's Whigs represented a social mix of White planters, merchants, lawyers, artisans and shopkeepers. Most of them owned slaves. The wealthiest owned scores or even hundreds. They found it difficult at first to gain the support of backcountry Whites, who were mainly small-scale farmers with few if any slaves. Backcountry folk had little interest in the economic and legal issues that occupied Lowcountry Whigs. Most had no burning grievance against the Crown, from whom they held their land grants. They were grossly underrepresented in a colonial assembly dominated by the merchant and planter elite. The assembly had failed to meet their demands for a working judicial system. Ethnic and religious differences further separated the two regions. The Lowcountry elite was predominately Anglican and Anglicized. The backcountry was heavily populated by Scotch-Irish, Scots, German and Welsh settlers. Lowcountry and backcountry resembled two adjoining countries with little love for one another. Once Lowcountry Whigs embraced confrontation with Britain, however, they had to convince backcountry Whites to join them. By 1775, there were more Whites in the backcountry than in the Lowcountry. The revolutionaries were extremely lucky that in the crucial months of that year the colony lacked effective royal leadership and a force of British soldiers that might have mobilized backcountry Whites for the Crown.

The road to revolution in South Carolina was paved with protests. Whigs protested the Stamp Act, the Townshend Acts, the Tea Act and the Coercion Acts. With each protest, the Whigs grew stronger, bolder, more confident. They had to create institutions to deal with each crisis. The Commons House of Assembly, the representative body of the colony, did not function for five years prior to the revolution due to the Wilkes Fund Controversy. In December 1769, the assembly allocated £1,500 to help English radical John Wilkes pay off debts incurred in his legal battles with royal authority. Despite his rakish reputation, Wilkes had become a hero to many American Whigs. The British government responded to the assembly's action by forbidding the colonial treasury to issue money without the signature of the royal governor. The directive deprived the assembly of its traditional control over money bills. It led to a power struggle between the assembly and Crown officials in which virtually nothing got done.

The Whigs established a series of extralegal committees to protest British policies and enforce nonimportation agreements. In July 1774, the Whig General Meeting elected five delegates to the First Continental Congress in Philadelphia. In November, the General Meeting called for the election of a Provincial Congress, which convened in Charleston in January 1775. The delegates elected planter Henry Laurens president and established committees to protect the "people's liberty" when it disbanded. The most important was the Secret Committee. The Congress directed the Secret Committee to do whatever it felt necessary for the defense and security of the colony. In April, the committee used this broad mandate to seize the colonial government's munitions and weaponry. This was more than a protest. It was an act of rebellion. A second Provincial Congress convened in early June. Its members voted to establish a provincial army and create an executive, the Council of Safety. The Congress removed all Crown appointees and replaced them with men "who had the confidence of the people." The delegates approved a document outlining the plan known as the Continental Association, or just the Association, which justified their resort to force in the defense of liberty. They called on all White men to sign it. Anyone who refused to sign would be designated an "obnoxious person inimical to the Liberty of the Colonies." South Carolina's revolution thus took place in 1775, a full year before the signing of the Declaration of Independence. As late as April, Whigs had spoken only of nonviolent protest. With some exceptions, they had not questioned the legitimacy of the royal government while neutering it in practice. Now they swept that government aside and declared themselves ready to fight against its domestic or foreign supporters. Men who had recently expressed horror at the idea of fighting their British brothers now declared themselves ready to die for the cause of freedom.

What brought about this radical transformation? The traditional view has been the arrival of news in early May that British troops had fired on the Massachusetts militia at Lexington and Concord. That had a significant effect. But more important were rumors accusing the British government of conspiring to incite slave insurrections and Indian attacks against colonial rebels. The panic the rumors aroused pushed conservative Whigs into the camp of radicals intent on removing the last shreds of British authority. What the defense of liberty could not convince them to do, the determination to maintain strict control over their human property did. The American war for liberty, especially in the southern colonies, was also a war to preserve slavery. In that sense the revolution had more in common with the Civil War than is generally acknowledged. Looked at from the perspective of the enslaved population, the revolution provided an opportunity to secure their liberty, not by fighting the British but by joining them. Historians estimate that around 100,000 enslaved persons ran off to British lines between 1775 and 1783. About a quarter of that number lived in South Carolina. They were not bystanders but active participants in the struggles that gave birth to a nation.

# ARTHUR MIDDLETON

Arthur Middleton is usually remembered as one of South Carolina's signers of the American Declaration of Independence, as a "Founding Father" of the United States. In the pivotal year 1775, he was one of the staunchest southern opponents of British colonial rule. That bland summation obscures a troubling reality about his actions and methods, not to mention the privileged position that made them possible. It is easy to forget that this signer of a declaration that proclaimed liberty and equality benefited from the labor of hundreds of enslaved Africans. Oddly, Middleton has not been the subject of a modern biography, but he left a trail in various documents and the writings of others. Charles Augustus Goodrich penned a brief narrative of Middleton's life in the 1820s in *Lives of the Signers of the Declaration of Independence*. Middleton was born in 1742 at The Oaks, his father's Goose Creek plantation. Henry Middleton also owned Middleton Place on the Ashley River, a popular tourist destination today. Like many of his plantocracy peers, Arthur received his formal education in England. He attended Harrow and Westminster schools and Trinity Hall Cambridge and studied law at the Middle Temple in London. Goodrich tells us that he excelled in classical studies and behaved like a choir boy. Avoiding the dissipated habits and "vicious indulgences" of his fellow students, he emerged as "an accomplished scholar and a moral man." After finishing his education, he took a Grand Tour of Europe lasting two years, polishing his taste in music, painting, sculpture and architecture. In 1763, he returned to South Carolina and married

Arthur Middleton and family by Benjamin West, 1771. *Courtesy, Middleton Place.*

Mary Izard. His father gave him Middleton Place and its human property. In 1765, he was elected to the Commons House of Assembly. He served in the assembly until 1768, when he and Mary went to England. They traveled extensively there and in France and Spain. While they were in England, the American-born artist Benjamin West painted a famous portrait of the Middletons with their infant son Henry. Ironically, West became a painter to the court of George III, whom Middleton would soon denounce as a tyrant.

The Middletons returned to South Carolina in 1771. At first, Arthur devoted himself to his plantation and horses, but by late 1774, he had emerged as one of the most outspoken opponents of British colonial policies. He joined the American Whigs. In April 1775, Middleton participated in Whig raids on Charleston's armory and powder magazines. The raids were a response to news that Virginia's royal governor, Lord Dunmore, had seized that colony's gunpowder and weapons to prevent them falling into rebellious hands. At this critical period, there was no royal governor in residence in South Carolina. The lieutenant governor, William Bull II, was acting governor. Bull was a South Carolina native connected to many of the elite by blood or marriage. The Whigs decided to preempt the possibility that he might follow Dunmore's lead. Their raids on the armory and powder magazines constituted a theft of Crown property. Bull had to respond, but in the absence of military force, he had little more than words to employ. He sent a message to the assembly, asking it to investigate the theft. Most of the assembly's members were members of the Provincial Congress. Many of them had taken part in the raids. Amid loud guffaws, Middleton moved they elect a committee of investigation, which they did. Two days later, the committee reported to more laughter that the raid had been the work of persons unknown, alarmed by the recent actions of the British government.

In June 1775, the second Provincial Congress appointed Middleton to the Council of Safety. According to Goodrich, "No one exhibited more activity, or manifested a greater degree of resolution and firmness, than did Arthur Middleton." He became known as the "Scourge of Loyalists" for harassing supporters of the British government, employing the Sons of Liberty as enforcers. In the spring of 1776, the Congress elected Middleton to the Second Continental Congress in Philadelphia. He replaced his father, Henry, who had resigned because he opposed independence. Arthur signed the Declaration of Independence with some reluctance. He feared it would lead to a British attack on Charleston. In fact, it had already happened. On June 28, a British fleet attacked the still unfinished harbor fort on Sullivan's Island. The Americans repulsed the enemy to win their first major victory of the war. The outcome of the battle increased enthusiasm for independence and made life more difficult for those who remained loyal to the Crown. Most of them kept a low profile. One who did not was the rector of St. Michael's, Robert Cooper. On the Sunday following the battle, Cooper offered the traditional prayers for the king. Bowing to Whig pressure, the church vestry dismissed him. He and many other Loyalists left during the next two years.

The British did not return in force to Carolina for nearly four years. During that time, the war raged in the northern and middle colonies. It barely affected Charleston except for rampant inflation and a couple of ill-fated attacks on British Florida. Middleton remained in Philadelphia until the end of 1777, when he resigned from Congress and returned to South Carolina. Goodrich states that he left with the reputation "of a man of the purest patriotism, of sound judgment, and unwavering resolution." Middleton was frustrated because Congress had refused his requests to increase military support for South Carolina. He believed he could accomplish more at home. Soon after his return, the state assembly voted a new constitution for South Carolina. President John Rutledge, who would have become governor under the new regime, refused his assent to the document and resigned. The assembly turned to Middleton, who also refused the job. Both believed the new constitution was too democratic. The assembly turned to another Lowcountry oligarch, Rawlins Lowndes, who had similar qualms, but he accepted.

In 1778, the British adopted a new strategy. The Southern Strategy, as it became known, rested on the belief that Loyalist sentiment was stronger in the Carolinas and Georgia than in colonies to the north. Exiled South Carolina Loyalists promoted the idea. Moses Kirkland, a backcountry Loyalist, had suggested it to Sir Henry Clinton, now the British commander in America. Clinton asked James Simpson, another South Carolina Loyalist, to investigate the strength of loyalism in the Carolinas and Georgia. Simpson reported that a British army could "expect to receive support from a large percentage of the inhabitants." Kirkland and Simpson overestimated the strength of southern loyalism. But after three years of failing to subdue the northern colonies, desperate British ministers leaped at the possibility of breaking the stalemate.

The Southern Strategy scored its first major success at the end of 1778. Clinton sent General Archibald Campbell and 2,500 British soldiers from New York to Georgia. Campbell linked up with General Augustine Prevost, commanding a British and Loyalist force from Florida. They captured Savannah just before Christmas. In the spring of 1779, American General Benjamin Lincoln, commanding in Charleston, marched the bulk of his army west to confront the British at Augusta. Sensing an opportunity, Prevost made a dash for Charleston. General Moultrie, commanding the force Lincoln left there, advanced to meet Prevost. Outnumbered, he ordered a retreat. Prevost reached the outskirts of the city but retreated when he learned that Lincoln's army was returning. In October, Prevost repulsed an American and French attempt to retake Savannah with great losses. In late December, another, much larger British army left New York, bound for Charleston. Clinton, who commanded the expedition, planned to land in South Carolina in the late autumn of 1779 to avoid the fever season, but the fleet's departure was delayed several times. After the ships set sail, severe winter storms dispersed them and lengthened the trip by several weeks. They reassembled off Savannah and sailed north. In February 1780, the army disembarked on Simmons (now Seabrook) Island. Joined by soldiers from Savannah, they advanced unopposed across the sea island marshes and swamps. They crossed the Ashley River at Bees Ferry

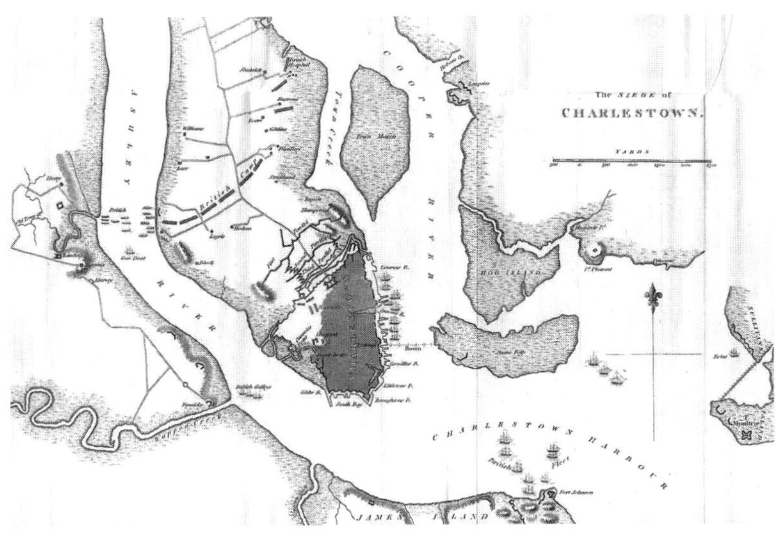


Map, Siege of Charleston, 1780. *From* Atlas to Marshall's Life of Washington.

at the end of March. They moved quickly down the Charleston peninsula and began to dig siege works. Meanwhile British warships entered the harbor, and other units closed off all routes of escape. After a siege of several weeks, Charleston's garrison surrendered on May 12.

For Middleton, the siege was a personal disaster. British soldiers sacked Middleton Place, beheading its statues, defacing its paintings and carting off many of its valuables. Middleton, a militia officer, was captured when the city surrendered. The British paroled the militia, which allowed them to go about their business, provided they took no active part in the war. A few weeks later, a spy informed the British commandant of Charleston, Lieutenant Colonel Nisbet Balfour, that Middleton and about twenty other rebels had been meeting secretly to plot further resistance. According to the spy, one of the attendees brought a pet baboon to their meetings dressed in a replica of a British uniform and called it "Colonel Balfour." Another, Peter Timothy, mocked the baboon as the ignorant son a Scottish bookseller. This was a reference to John Wells, son of Timothy's former printing rival, Loyalist Robert Wells. Balfour arrested Middleton and about twenty others for violating their parole and shipped them to St. Augustine. The following July, the British sent them to Philadelphia as part of a prisoner exchange. Middleton served in the Continental Congress until the war ended and then returned to

South Carolina. Voters elected him to the state assembly in 1785 and 1786. A malignant fever ended his political career and life in January 1787. His political legacy was mixed. His devotion to the Whig cause was firm. His obituary in the *State Gazette of South Carolina* describes Middleton as "a tender husband and parent, humane master, steady unshaken patriot, the gentleman and the scholar." A more complete summation of his life must include the reality that his actions and his life violated the principles of liberty and equality he espoused in signing the Declaration of Independence.

# WILLIAM HENRY DRAYTON

William Henry Drayton was one of the most active and energetic of the Charleston revolutionaries. He was born into aristocratic privilege in 1742. His birthplace, Drayton Hall, is a grand Neo-Palladian mansion about fifteen miles up the Ashley River from Charleston. Drayton's father, John, built it from the profits of rice planting. William Henry went to England at age ten to be educated at Westminster School and Balliol College, Oxford. After he came home in 1764, the South Carolina Bar admitted him to practice of the law. He married Dorothy Golightly, a wealthy heiress, the same year. In the following years, he squandered much of their fortune on gambling.

Drayton began his political odyssey as a staunch defender of British rule. He was elected to the colonial assembly after his return to South Carolina and supported Parliament's right to pass the Stamp Act. Angry electors rejected him at the next election. Undeterred, in 1769 he wrote an inflammatory article opposing the Non-Importation Agreement, which called for a colonial embargo on British goods. He declared the agreement illegal and designed "to ruin and overthrow our happy constitution." Supporters of the agreement ostracized Drayton socially and economically. Christopher Gadsden called him a lunatic. Seeking to improve his financial position, he sailed to England in 1770 in quest of royal patronage. The Crown appointed him to the governor's council of South Carolina but failed to give him what he really wanted: a lucrative job in the colony's royal administration. Most of those posts went to native

Britons. Drayton's disappointment turned to fury when John Stuart, superintendent for Indian affairs in the southern colonies, prevented him from concluding a fraudulent land deal with the Catawba Nation. Since the Crown had appointed him in the early 1760s, Stuart had been trying to protect the southern tribes from rapacious land speculators. "I know of nothing so likely to interrupt and disturb our tranquillity with the Indians," he reported, "as the incessant attempts to defraud them of their land by clandestine purchase." The struggle between Stuart and Drayton was essentially between an imperial bureaucrat determined to achieve central control of frontier policy and a provincial aristocrat who resented interference with his actions. Frustrated by these obstacles to his ambitions, Drayton rearranged his political loyalties. The imperial government he had praised became the enemy. He defended his reversal by arguing that he was consistent in his principles but circumstances had changed. The government in London was now the greatest threat to the "happy constitution." Crown minsters were corrupting a "balanced political system" dominated by the local elite by elevating British "placemen" to positions of power. Once converted, Drayton became one of the most zealous of the Whigs.

In the summer of 1774, Drayton published an incendiary pamphlet displaying his Whig credentials. *A Letter from Freeman* was a manifesto of American rights. It denounced the British government as "tyrannical" and the Coercion Acts as "malignant." The local villain became a local hero. Voters elected him to the First Provincial Congress. The *Letter* and Drayton's exhortations to grand juries to "choose freedom over slavery" and reject British rule outraged Crown officials. Stuart and other members of the council demanded Drayton's suspension from that body for attempting to "subvert the constitution." Acting governor William Bull, Drayton's uncle, suspended him in March 1775. By then, Drayton had emerged as a leader of the radical Whigs in the Provincial Congress. The Congress appointed him to several committees, including the powerful Secret Committee, which elected him chair. Other members included Arthur Middleton and Edward Weyman, leader of the Sons of Liberty. Together, they mobilized support for the incipient rebellion and intimidated opponents and the uncommitted.

Under Drayton's leadership, the Secret Committee directed the raid on the colony's armory and powder magazines in April. Drayton followed with measures designed to arouse popular anger against Britain. He commissioned the Liberty Boys to construct a wheeled and curtained tableau displaying

William Henry Drayton, etching, circa 1779. *U.S. National Portrait Gallery.*

effigies of the pope, the devil and two British prime ministers. They set it up at the busy intersection of Meeting and Broad Streets. The prime ministers were Lord Grenville of Stamp Act infamy, who had been dead for five years, and the current prime minister, Lord North. Grenville held up a bag labeled "STAMPS." North was recognizable from his crossed eyes. The figures of the prime ministers were immovable and kneeling, facing the pope. The effigies of the pope and devil were moved by two men hidden in the curtained part below. The pope held a boot, a symbol of tyranny representing a third prime minister, Lord Bute. Whenever supporters of the British government walked past, the pope would bow respectfully toward them. The devil then responded by aiming his dart at the pope's head, to the delight of people gathered to watch. The intended message was that the pope and British government were outdoing the devil in wickedness. At the end of the day, a crowd paraded the contraption around town and burned the effigies. Drayton claimed the affair had recruited many young men to the cause of liberty.

In early July, Drayton led a raid on the Charleston Post Office. He arrived with two other men one evening after the office had closed for the day. The assistant postmaster, Jervis Henry Stevens, was there sorting mail. Drayton knocked and asked to be admitted. Stevens told him to come back the next day. Drayton threatened to break down the door, and Stevens let him in. Drayton took away dispatches from London intended for the royal governors of the Carolinas, Georgia and Florida. The letters included instructions to consider using Indian and Black auxiliaries if necessary to combat colonial rebellion. Drayton and his allies spread the news widely. Added to other rumors of British perfidy, the revelations increased the anxiety of many Charlestonians to a fever pitch. They also strengthened the hands of those encouraging "liberty mobs" to hound officials and supporters of the British government.

A key target of Drayton's wrath was Colonel John Stuart. Although Drayton denounced Stuart as a placeman lacking local connections, he had been in Charleston since 1748. He married a wealthy heiress, Sarah Fenwick, became a planter and involved himself in public affairs. He served as a militia captain in the Cherokee War of 1760. The Cherokee captured him, but a headman who befriended him, Attakullakulla, helped him escape. In 1762, the Crown appointed Stuart to the post of superintendent of Indian affairs for the Southern District. Stuart was popular among the Native nations of the Southeast, but his efforts to protect their lands from settler encroachment made him enemies among the colonists. Drayton conducted what can only be called a vendetta against him. He accused Stuart of orchestrating Indian attacks on the colony. The opposite was true. Stuart was trying to keep the southern tribes neutral. He believed that their involvement in the dispute between Britain and its colonies would be disastrous for everybody. At the same time, he was trying to keep them friendly toward Britain. The hysteria about Indian attacks and slave uprisings made his position untenable. The Council of Safety ordered Stuart's arrest in early June. Warned by friends of his danger, Stuart fled from his Tradd Street house at night and went to Savannah. The council instructed Georgia Whigs to arrest Stuart and send him back to Charleston. Once again, someone alerted Stuart to his danger. He narrowly escaped arrest and took a ship to St. Augustine. In his letter to the council, Stuart claimed that Drayton had smeared him in revenge. Drayton was furious. He spread the news of Stuart's "treachery" widely and portrayed Stuart as a spider at the center of a web of British plots against the colonies. The Whigs placed Stuart's wife, Sarah, under house arrest as a hostage for his good behavior. She remained there for nearly a year. In May 1776, she escaped or was released into the hands of Creek emissaries, who escorted her to her husband. By then, Stuart was in Pensacola, West Florida, managing relations with the Creeks and Choctaws. He died there in 1779.

In the late summer of 1775, the Council of Safety sent Drayton on a mission to the South Carolina backcountry. The council instructed him to inform the people there about the issues at stake in the dispute between Britain and its colonies and "to force the necessity of a general union, in order to preserve themselves and their children from slavery." The mission was dictated by demographic reality: by 1775, the White population of the backcountry was larger than that of the Lowcountry. Most of the backcountry colonists had little interest in the issues that spurred Lowcountry Whigs to rebellion. Many were inclined to support the British government that had granted them land. If the backcountry remained loyal, the Lowcountry rebellion had little chance of success. Drayton's mission triggered a political chess game with no settled rules. His party included two clergyman, Presbyterian William

Tennent and Baptist Oliver Hart. The council included them because most of the backcountry settlers were Presbyterians or Baptists, whereas Drayton and the Lowcountry elite were mainly Anglican. Tennent rivaled Drayton in extreme rhetoric. He accused Loyalists of planning the "devastation of the whole province," hatching "a hellish plot" and "preparing a great dish of blood for you."

Initially, Drayton's delegation met with little success in persuading backcountry folks to sign the Association. The "Dutch" (Germans) of the Midlands were almost unanimously opposed, fearing the king might revoke their land grants. After trying in vain to recruit them, Drayton confessed, "The Germans are not with us." The other ethnic groups were divided. Many backcountry settlers were inclined to support the Crown or simply confused about the issues. Several militia leaders stymied Drayton's efforts at every opportunity, notably Robert Cunningham, Moses Kirkland and Thomas Brown. They exploited the widespread backcountry belief that no one from Charleston could be trusted or believed. The Lowcountry elite's condescending attitude toward backcountry folk did not help the Whig cause. In a letter to Drayton during the early stages of the mission, Arthur Middleton wrote that he was "sorry to hear you have been under a necessity of exercising your abilities upon the soldiery by sermons and harangues. I wish you may not have thrown your jewels among swine." Middleton argued that persuasion would not be enough. The sword might be necessary.

Drayton responded with more aggressive tactics. He tried to capture or kill the several Loyalist leaders without success. He mustered a pro-Whig militia force and confronted Loyalist militia at the town of Ninety-Six. Using a combination of bribes, bluff, threats and violence, he persuaded timorous and probably drunken Loyalist Colonel Thomas Fletchall to agree to a one-sided truce on September 16. Fletchall pledged that the king's supporters would not assist any British attack on the colony or oppose the proceedings of the Provincial Congress. In return, Drayton promised that men who refused to sign the Association would not be molested. Cunningham and Brown denounced the truce as "false and disgraceful." Cunningham accused Drayton of underhanded tactics, browbeating Fletchall and scaring men out of their wits at the "sight of liberty caps and the sound of cannon." The Treaty of Ninety-Six, as the truce became known, bought the Whigs time. They violated its terms almost immediately. At Drayton's insistence, the Council of Safety ordered the arrest of Loyalist militia leaders who had refused to sign the treaty. Kirkland and Brown escaped the net and served the British in various capacities during the war. The council imprisoned Cunningham and several others on a charge of having committed high crimes and misdemeanors against the liberties of South Carolina. They were released a few months later, but Cunningham did not forgive or forget. In 1780, he joined the British and rose to become a brigadier general.

Returning to Charleston, Drayton gave a "talk" to a group of Cherokee headmen at the Congaree Store, a trading post in the Midlands. Tensions between the southern tribes and backcountry settlers were sharpening because of White encroachment on the tribes' hunting lands. Shady speculators continued their attempts to cheat the Indians of their lands, plying them with rum before getting them to sign deeds they did not understand. In 1774, Thomas Fee had murdered a Creek leader who had come to Augusta to discuss peace. The royal governor of Georgia ordered Fee arrested and sent to the jail at Ninety-Six, but a mob stormed the jail and freed him. More recently, an unidentified White man had killed a Cherokee and wounded two others in Georgia. The headmen demanded justice. Drayton's "talk" to them was like one he had given several weeks before to leaders of the Catawba Nation. The Catawba were already inclined to support the Whigs, but Drayton threatened them with severe reprisals should they join the British. The Catawba sent warriors to fight for the Whigs. Serving as rangers, they helped track down runaway slaves and Loyalists. In effect, the Whigs did what they falsely accused Stuart of doing.

The Catawba were a small tribe with fewer than a hundred warriors. The Cherokee were a much larger nation and favorably disposed toward the British. Drayton tried to convince the Cherokee headmen that the British government had been corrupted by wicked men who had misled the king. These "evil councilors" were pursuing policies that hurt the colonists and the Indians who traded with them. "They persuade the Great King to charge us more for our goods. That's a bad thing for you as well. If we must pay him more for our goods, you'll have to pay us more for yours." The colonists had refused to pay, and the evil councilors were sending soldiers to enforce payment. The British soldiers had killed "our people" in Boston. They might soon come to Carolina, "killing our men, and enslaving our women and children. If they treat us, their own flesh and blood, in this bad way, what can the Cherokee expect from them?" The colonists were preparing to defend themselves. If they succeeded, the Cherokee would benefit from cheap and plentiful goods. They did not need to fight in this "white man's quarrel." But if they fought for the British, he warned, the Whigs would destroy their towns. He ended on a conciliatory note. "We do not believe the bad talk that says you want to be our enemies. We want you to be our brothers, so take my good talk to heart." The headmen found Drayton's "talk" condescending. One accused him of treating them like children. "We know the whites may fight each other. Stuart's agents have told us. They wish us to stay out of it. That is our wish, too." But he added a warning of his own: their young men were furious because Whites continued to move onto Cherokee lands. "You must stop cheating our people and taking our lands if you want peace."

Drayton failed to detach the Cherokee from their British allegiance, mainly because of continued settler encroachment on their lands. He did agree to send them powder and lead for the hunting season. After he returned to Charleston, the Council of Safety approved a shipment of munitions to the Cherokee. This was a risky move given the Whigs had aroused fears of Indian attacks. The decision angered many backcountry people, who feared the Cherokee would use the munitions against them. Loyalists encouraged that belief. It helped them recruit a force that seized the shipment and marched to Ninety-Six. Whig militia pursued them. The two sides alternated fighting and negotiating for several days before concluding a truce on November 22. A month later, a much larger Whig force defeated the Loyalist militia and seized many of their leaders. The Whig victory eliminated the Loyalist threat in South Carolina for four years.

In November, the Provincial Congress elected Drayton president. The original president, Henry Laurens, resigned, hoping that the presidency would moderate Drayton. Instead, he became more radical. In March 1776, he shocked the Congress by moving that it declare independence from Great Britain. The majority voted against the motion, but the seed was planted. Later that month, the Congress declared South Carolina an independent state until an accommodation could be reached with Great Britain. The Congress approved a provisional constitution for the state. The Provincial Congress was renamed the General Assembly. The Council of Safety ceased to exist. The assembly chose John Rutledge as president and Drayton as chief justice. Drayton used the bench as a bully pulpit.

In early July 1776, Cherokee bands led by Dragging Canoe attacked White settlers in the Carolina backcountry, killing about sixty. Stuart and his Cherokee agent Alexander Cameron had tried to dissuade Dragging Canoe. Whig leaders blamed them anyway. Henry Laurens predicted that the names Stuart and Cameron would "forever be detestable in Carolina." In what became known as the Second Cherokee War, southern militias burned more than fifty Cherokee towns and destroyed their crops in reprisal. Most of the Cherokee soon made peace. Dragging Canoe and his followers moved west and continued to fight, now encouraged by British agents. Drayton played to the popular thirst for vengeance. Every captured Cherokee, he wrote, "should become the property of the taker." The Cherokee Nation should be "extirpated" and their lands given to Americans. The peace settlement forced them to surrender nearly all their land in South Carolina. A small number of Loyalists were captured fighting with the Cherokee. A Whig court convicted them of treason and sentenced them to hang. Drayton remarked that he would have hanged them without trial to save the state money. Rutledge, who continued to hope for a negotiated settlement with Britain, pardoned them. In a published charge to a grand jury around the same time, Drayton declared that God had chosen the "American Empire" to replace Great Britain as his tool to advance the cause of liberty. God had previously chosen Britain, but the British had violated His intentions by "trying to enslave the American people." Apparently, God lacked a sense of irony. Drayton claimed that the British government had forced South Carolina to choose between independence or slavery. In reality, South Carolina's Whigs chose independence *and* slavery.

After the Cherokee War of 1776, Drayton helped draft a new state constitution, which the state assembly approved in March 1778. Later that year, the assembly elected him to the Continental Congress in Philadelphia. In that role, he took part in drawing up the first constitution of the United States, the Articles of Confederation. He tried to undermine its already weak central executive power, opposed attempts to reach a compromise with the British government and defended "southern interests"—a phrase already becoming a euphemism for slavery. He clashed with other delegates, including Henry Laurens, then president of the Continental Congress. In September 1779, he succumbed to a "bilious" fever in Philadelphia. He was only thirty-seven. In modern political terms, Drayton was a populist—that is, someone who appeals to people who believe elites have ignored their concerns. In 1775, he enlisted "the people" to defend the "happy constitution." That did not make him a democrat or an innovator, except in demanding independence. The best government, he believed, was government by a propertied and "disinterested" aristocracy, people like himself and, ironically, the men who governed Britain.

# CHRISTOPHER GADSDEN

Christopher Gadsden is best known today as the designer of the iconic "Gadsden flag." The flag features a rattlesnake on a bright yellow background, with the words "DONT TREAD ON ME" at the bottom. The snake is coiled to strike. The flag was intended as a warning to the British government: step on American liberty at your peril. The snake has thirteen rattles, symbolizing the thirteen colonies. Gadsden presented the flag to the Provincial Congress in February 1776. He had just returned from serving in the Continental Congress. The delegates cheered the flag. They were less enthusiastic about a pamphlet he brought, written by a recent arrival from England, *Common Sense.* Its author, Thomas Paine, called for independence. Many delegates cried, "Never!" Rawlins Lowndes denounced Paine as a demagogue. John Rutledge declared that to advocate independence from Great Britain was treasonous.

Today the Gadsden flag is better known than its designer, who nonetheless played a significant part in the revolution. Christopher Gadsden was born in Charleston, South Carolina, in 1724. His father, Thomas, was a former British naval officer the Crown appointed as customs collector for the port of Charleston. Thomas sent Christopher to Bristol, England, a major slave trading port, to be educated and trained as a merchant. Returning to America in 1740, he worked briefly as an apprentice in a Philadelphia counting house before returning to Charleston. He inherited a sizeable fortune when his parents died in 1741. During King George's War (1744–48) he served as a purser on a British

Gadsden flag. *Wikimedia Commons.*

naval vessel, making purchases and keeping accounts. After the war, he became a factor, receiving and storing goods for other merchants. In 1767, he built a wharf in Charleston, one of the largest in any American port. Gadsden's Wharf became a major entry point into the city for the enslaved. More than 100,000 Africans disembarked there between 1767 and 1808, when the legal slave trade ended.

During the construction of his wharf, Gadsden remarked that he was going to "fill the foundation with imported Scotchmen, who are fit for nothing better." The statement reflected his dislike of Scots, particularly Scottish merchants, who he viewed as undeserving beneficiaries of British trade policies. Gadsden had displayed open hostility toward Scots years before while serving as a militia officer during the Cherokee War of 1760. South Carolina requested the British government send soldiers to quell the Cherokee uprising. To Gadsden's dismay, they sent a regiment of Scottish Highlanders and gave command to their officers. Gadsden believed a South Carolinian should lead the campaign. His resentment of Scots was shared by other colonials. A couple of years earlier, the arrival of colonial soldiers and Highlanders had led to a bitter conflict. South Carolina had asked for soldiers to defend them against French attack but had not prepared housing for them. Their commander, Colonel Henry Bouquet, demanded that Charlestonians house the soldiers to protect them against fevers. Although some people did comply, most of Bouquet's men were left to camp outside close to the wharves, where yellow fever lurked. Scores died of illness.

In the decade before the revolution, Scottophobia had developed in tandem with anger at the actions of the British government. Whigs on both sides of the Atlantic claimed the two were linked, that Scots dominated the government in London and were conspiring to undermine English liberties. Gadsden's hero John Wilkes was a major disseminator of the Scottish conspiracy theory. At the time he was building his wharf, Gadsden was developing the area near Boundary (Calhoun) Street. He called it Middlesex and named one of the streets after Wilkes, member of Parliament for the English county of Middlesex. Channeling Wilkes, Gadsden called the Scots of Charleston "cunning, Jacobitical, Butean rascals" who did everything they could to undermine efforts "of the true sons of liberty among us."

Gadsden had served in the Commons House of Assembly since 1757. He used his position there and the newspapers to oppose British efforts to control the colonies. His defense of colonial rights derived from his concept of the rights of Englishmen, which he grounded in natural rights philosophy. Whereas the Crown claimed that it granted rights to the colonies, Gadsden countered that the rights were inherent in nature. His argument echoed that of English philosopher John Locke. Ten years before the Declaration of Independence, Gadsden claimed the colonies were sovereign. He denounced the Stamp Act, which he viewed as a violation of colonial rights, as taxation without representation. The South Carolina Assembly appointed him to represent them at the Stamp Act Congress in New York City. Gadsden was one of the most uncompromising delegates. He formed an alliance with Sam Adams, leader of Boston's Sons of Liberty. In 1766, a new administration bowed to colonial anger and repealed the Stamp Act. To save face, Parliament followed the repeal with an act declaring it retained the right to legislate for the colonies. Two years later, Parliament approved new taxes. The Townshend Duties placed taxes on glass, paint, paper, lead and tea. Colonial resistance through the Non-Importation Movement led Parliament to retreat and repeal all the duties except a tiny tax on tea. The Tea Act of 1773 was designed to help the cash-strapped East India Company, which received a virtual monopoly of the tea trade to the colonies.

The most famous colonial reaction to the Tea Act was the Boston Tea Party. In December 1773, Boston's Sons of Liberty boarded a merchant ship bringing a consignment of tea to the city and tossed it into the harbor. Parliament responded with the Coercion or "Intolerable" Acts, which were designed to punish Massachusetts and frighten the other colonies into submission. Instead, they led to greater colonial cooperation against British policies. Twelve colonies, all but Georgia, sent delegates to the First Continental Congress in Philadelphia. Gadsden was one of five South Carolina delegates at the Congress, which met in the autumn of 1774. The Congress proposed to protest British policies through an embargo on British goods. The document justifying the plan, known simply as the Association, accused the British government of trying to enslave the colonies. Congress chose an economic boycott as their tool of resistance because they believed it would be effective and nonviolent. In fact, it often led to violence. To succeed, the embargo required widespread cooperation from merchants and consumers. The Congress urged colonies to establish committees to encourage citizens to sign the Association, in effect to pledge allegiance to the resistance movement. Some people signed willingly. Others refused or hesitated to do so, viewing it as treasonous. To convince them to sign, radical Whigs, aided by the Sons of Liberty, used coercion, including ostracism, intimidation and mob action.

Charleston had not one but three tea parties. They lacked the drama of the Boston event, but they made the same point. The first took place a week before Boston's. On December 1, 1773, the merchant ship *London* arrived in Charleston with a large consignment of tea. Gadsden called a "Mass Meeting" of local Whigs and Liberty Boys. The attendees discussed how to prevent the sale of the tea. They interrogated the three merchants who had agreed to receive the consignment. After "threats and flattery" they persuaded the merchants not to receive the tea. They threatened the captain of the *London* and the owner of the wharf where it was anchored. The collector of customs ended the standoff when he seized the tea and put it in the bottom floor of the Exchange. He declared it would remain there until Parliament resolved the tax dispute. Despite the threats, no violence occurred. It was a genteel affair compared to that in Boston, a fact that angered local firebrands. They were upset that the tea had entered the city at all, especially after they learned what happened in Boston, Philadelphia and New York City. In the latter two cities, Whig activists prevented the tea-laden ships from landing. They returned their cargoes to Britain.

Charleston's second tea party was a rougher affair that reveals what the earlier threats may have been. It took place in July 1774. A merchant ship called, ironically, the *Magna Carta* arrived carrying a mere three crates of tea. Its captain registered the tea with customs officials at the Exchange. After the first tea party, members of the Mass Meeting had created a General

Committee to enforce the prohibition on the import of taxed tea. The committee summoned the captain and demanded an explanation. Captain Maitland claimed he was unaware his ship was carrying tea when it sailed and only discovered its presence once at sea. He offered to dump the tea into the harbor at his own cost. The General Committee accepted his explanation and approved his solution, but customs officers refused to let him pay the duty on the tea. The Liberty Boys concluded that Maitland was being duplicitous. They aroused a mob of several hundred citizens and set out with tar and feathers to teach him a painful lesson. Maitland learned of their approach and escaped to another ship in the harbor. The mob found the tea on his ship and took it to the Exchange.

The third Charleston tea party was nonviolent but more like Boston's in that it involved dumping tea into the harbor. In November 1774, the ship that rescued Maitland, *Britannia*, arrived carrying seven chests of tea. The captain, Samuel Ball, repeated Maitland's excuse, claiming that he did not know of the presence of the "mischievous drug" on his ship. Ball was not being truthful, but the General Committee accepted his explanation and blamed the three Charleston merchants who had agreed to accept consignments of tea. The committee persuaded them to dump the tea into the Cooper River at a loss to themselves. The memory of the mob chasing Maitland may have helped convince them. A large crowd gathered to watch them pour the tea into the harbor. Peter Timothy reported the event in his *South Carolina Gazette*, calling the tea dumping "an oblation to Neptune."

Gadsden encouraged such extralegal actions. In March 1775, he led a liberty mob to the docks to stop a ship unloading horses and furniture arriving from Britain. The Committee of Safety had given the purchaser permission to import them because they were for his personal use, not for sale. Gadsden threatened to shoot the horses if they were unloaded. The committee retreated in the face of this mob action and reversed its position. Gadsden acknowledged that such actions might cause harm to some individuals, but inaction, he argued, was the greater danger. The alternative to defending liberty was to submit to slavery, to sink to the level of plantation slaves. Irony aside, this was compelling rhetoric. In the early 1770s, it became commonplace among American Whigs to accuse the British government of attempting to enslave them. Northern Whigs adopted the metaphor as a means of uniting the colonies. To southern Whigs surrounded by the enslaved, it was more than a metaphor. They had an acute sense of what losing one's liberty meant: to be reduced to property, stripped of humanity and rights. That did not make them sympathetic to the enslaved, as Blacks who had the audacity to seek their own liberty soon discovered.

In May 1775, Gadsden returned to Philadelphia as a delegate to the second Continental Congress. On this occasion, Georgia sent delegates, and twelve colonies became thirteen. Fighting had already broken out in Massachusetts. In January 1776, hearing that Charleston expected an imminent British attack, Gadsden left Philadelphia to assume command of the newly formed First South Carolina Regiment. On that occasion, he presented his rattlesnake flag to the Provincial Congress. Following independence, President Rutledge appointed Gadsden as a brigadier general. Gadsden clashed with General Robert Howe, the Continental army commander in the South. In 1777, he challenged Howe to a duel. Howe fired first and missed. Gadsden fired widely on purpose. With his honor preserved, Gadsden resigned his military commission. He continued to serve in the State Assembly. In 1778, he helped Drayton draft a new state constitution. Under it, Rawlins Lowndes became governor. Gadsden became lieutenant governor. In that position, he had an epiphany. He began to doubt the wisdom of inciting violent popular action. He defended Lowndes's efforts to restrain his former allies, the Liberty Boys, who were threatening the hegemony of the elite.

By the time the British laid siege to Charleston in the spring of 1780, John Rutledge had replaced Lowndes as governor. Rutledge left for the backcountry to rally resistance. Lieutenant Governor Gadsden stayed to help with the defense of the city. General Benjamin Lincoln, leader of the southern Continental army since October 1778, commanded the defensive forces. Lincoln ordered the erection of defensive earthworks and the digging of a moat to the north of the city. The defenders were short of supplies and equipment, including artillery. Poor morale, indiscipline and low enlistments hampered their efforts. The legislature had tried to increase the number of soldiers through a combination of inducements and repression. In 1778, it passed the Vagrant Act, which allowed the authorities to impress men wandering about, begging or otherwise unemployed in useful labor. The assembly offered land grants and other bounties to men who enlisted voluntarily. Desertion from the army was a frequent problem, met by hangings and severe floggings. A smallpox epidemic that broke out in Charleston in the autumn of 1779 made recruiting from the backcountry even more difficult. Most rural folk lacked immunity to the deadly scourge, and few men were willing to risk infection. Slaves forced to work on the defensive works were also vulnerable. Many of them died from smallpox. The rest were taken out of town until the epidemic ran its course.

The British plan of attack caught the defenders by surprise. Instead of attacking the fort on Sullivan's Island as in 1776, Sir Henry Clinton bypassed it and the other harbor defenses. He landed his army unmolested about twenty-five miles southwest at Simmons Island (now Seabrook). At the end of March, they crossed the Ashley River and moved down the Charleston peninsula. Within days, they were constructing siege lines. Meanwhile, British warships had entered the harbor. Lincoln concluded that defeat was inevitable. He proposed to escape with his army while escape was possible. Gadsden was furious when he got word of Lincoln's plan. He stormed into the general's headquarters as Lincoln was presenting the case for evacuation to his officers. Gadsden accused Lincoln of cowardice. Gadsden's councilors and a crowd of angry citizens followed him into the room. One of them threatened to open the gates to the British and join them in attacking Lincoln's men before they got to their boats. Most of Lincoln's South Carolina officers pressed him to remain and fight "to the last extremity," for "liberty or death." The French officers present supported Lincoln. General Moultrie proposed that the army remain and reassess the situation in a few days. Lincoln reluctantly agreed. By then, the army was trapped. On April 14, a British detachment led by Lieutenant Colonel Banastre Tarleton routed Isaac Huger's cavalry at the Battle of Monck's Corner, which cut off Lincoln's last escape route. Clinton offered terms of surrender. Lincoln refused several times and proposed his own, which

*Siege of Charleston* (1780) by Alonzo Chappel, painted circa 1862. *Brown University Library.*

included being able to march his army away unmolested, along with their arms and supplies. Certain of victory, Clinton rejected such a concession. On May 10, the British unleashed a sustained artillery barrage on the city, setting many houses on fire.

Gadsden led another delegation to Lincoln's headquarters. This time he demanded that Lincoln surrender to save lives and property. Lincoln accepted Clinton's terms. On May 12, the entire American army of more than five thousand men became prisoners of war. More people died on the day of surrender than during the entire siege, but not from battle. As the Americans were surrendering their weapons at the powder magazine on Magazine Street, the powder exploded, killing scores and injuring hundreds. The dead and wounded included soldiers from both sides, women from a nearby brothel and most of the "poor lunatics" at the adjacent poorhouse and hospital. Each side blamed the other for what was most likely a tragic accident. The explosion was probably caused when a soldier threw down a loaded musket that discharged into the magazine.

The British paroled Gadsden. But he was arrested several weeks later, along with some twenty others, for violating his parole and sent to St. Augustine. On their arrival, the British commandant offered them the freedom of the town. Gadsden alone refused it. The British sent them to Philadelphia in the summer of 1781. Gadsden returned to South Carolina in early 1782 and served in the assembly that met in Jacksonborough that February. The assembly convened there because Charleston remained under British occupation. The delegates elected him governor, but he declined on grounds of poor health. He had another surprise for them. It related to one of the most contentious items on the assembly's agenda: what to do with Loyalists after the war. Unlike previous South Carolina assemblies, most of the delegates were from the backcountry. Bent on revenge, they demanded that Loyalists receive severe punishment. Gadsden shocked them by urging leniency. "Revenge is not manly," he said. "Leave it to God." He asked them to discriminate. Many people who submitted to the British in 1780, he argued, did nothing worse than submit to a superior force and try to resume a normal life. Only those who actively persecuted and plundered their Patriot neighbors should be punished. Others should be forgiven to heal the wounds of division in the new country. His words had a negligible effect on most of the delegates. They shouted him down, relating tales of Loyalist atrocities. One bragged about how many Loyalists he had killed. Others shouted things

Christopher Gadsden. Charles Fraser, miniature, 1805. *Gibbes Museum of Art.*

like "We've been ruined by this war! It's our turn to get our due! The Tories must bleed! They're fat sheep! Prick 'em! Yes, prick 'em!" Some delegates accused Gadsden of trying to protect Loyalist relatives and friends.

Gadsden's stance reflected how the war had changed him. He had once encouraged the threatening and violent behavior of the Liberty Boys. Now he denounced mob action and disorder. In one crucial respect, he had not changed. He remained insensitive to the disconnect between his demands for liberty and his ownership of other human beings. In this, of course, he was hardly alone. In postwar South Carolina, questioning slavery became even more rare than before independence. Once deemed a necessary evil, it became viewed as a positive good. In the aftermath of the war, Gadsden retreated from politics, except for serving in the state convention of 1788 that ratified the United States Constitution. For the most part, he lived quietly at a house he had built on East Bay Street, still known as the Gadsden House. He died in 1805 after falling from a horse.

# GEORGE MILLIGEN

Likely few people have heard of George Milligen. Yet he was one of the most vocal supporters of the British government in South Carolina on the eve of the American Revolution. Milligen was born in Scotland around 1720. After training as a surgeon, he joined the British army in 1745. He came to South Carolina in 1753 as surgeon to his majesty's forces in South Carolina and Georgia, a title grander in name than reality. The number of British soldiers and sailors in the two southern provinces was tiny. In 1759, Milligen accompanied Governor William Henry Lyttleton's disastrous punitive expedition against the Cherokee. It produced the Cherokee War of 1760 and unleashed a smallpox epidemic across South Carolina. A few years later, Milligen wrote *A Short Description of the Province of South-Carolina: With an Account of the Air, Weather, and Diseases of Charles-Town* (1763). The American Philosophical Society elected him a member in 1772. Before the crisis in colonial-British relations, he was an active member of the Charleston community, a Mason involved in civic and philanthropic affairs.

As a Crown appointee with a strong sense of duty and loyalty, Milligen viewed the drift toward revolution with alarm. The Sons of Liberty pressured him to sign the Association. He not only refused but also questioned the legitimacy of the Provincial Congress. The Council of Safety summoned him to explain himself. Henry Laurens, the council president, asked Milligen if he agreed that the colonists "possessed the rights and liberties of Englishmen." Milligen replied, "I support the civil and religious rights of mankind." His answer articulated the natural rights philosophy that would appear in the Declaration of Independence a year later. He may also have been taking a dig at Laurens. In saying "mankind" instead of "Englishmen," Milligen was essentially telling Laurens, "I have a broader conception of rights than you." At the time, Laurens and his colleagues were denying that an African, Thomas Jeremiah, was entitled to the same rights as Whites. Laurens then asked Milligen if he considered himself a patriot. "I do," Milligen answered. "Then why can't you stand with us?" Laurens continued. Milligen had obviously prepared his answer: "For me, patriotism includes support for the king, protector of the rights and liberties of his subjects. For thirty years, I have served His Majesty as a soldier and a surgeon and eaten his bread. Allegiance as a subject, gratitude as a man, honour as a gentleman, and my duty to the king all forbid my joining your Association." Laurens dismissed Milligen and asked him to appear before the council again on August 15.

Milligen's outspokenness made him a special target of the Sons of Liberty. Two leading Liberty Boys, Daniel Cannon and Edward Weyman, threatened Milligen that if he did not sign, he should "expect to be treated agreeable to the rules of sound policy." Several days before, a liberty mob had treated two Irishmen, James Dealey and Laughlin Martin, according to said rules. A third man, Michael Hubart, who worked on the wharves, had denounced them to the Sons of Liberty. Hubart claimed he had gone to Nicoll's Tavern after work. Dealey came in soon after and asked the patrons in a loud voice if they had heard the "good news" that King George was shipping thousands of guns to the colonies to arm the "Negroes, Indians, and Roman Catholics." Hubart called Dealey a blackguard for cheering news of a plan that could lead to the massacre of good Christian folk. Dealey looked at him fiercely, thumped his chest and proclaimed, 'I'm a Roman Catholic! I have arms, I'll get more arms, and I'll use 'em as I please!" Hubart left Nicoll's to go home, fearing that Dealey was mad. Dealey followed him, joined by two others: Laughlin Martin and a man named Reed. They were drunk, Hubart claimed. They entered his house, sat down and stared at him angrily. Martin blurted out, "So, Hubart, you'll not allow Roman Catholics to carry guns?" Hubart replied that he didn't have the power to forbid anyone from carrying guns. Martin cursed him, called him a false-faced villain and told Dealey to take him outside and cut him to pieces. Dealey dragged him out to the street and grabbed his throat. Reed intervened and forced Dealey to release Hubart, saying, "This has gone far enough." Martin came out, "mad with drink," holding a large knife in his hand. He placed it near Hubart's throat and threatened to cut off his head unless he begged pardon from Dealey. Hubart begged Dealey's pardon, and his assailants left. It is impossible to judge the veracity of Hubart's story. One thing we do know is that Dealey's "good news," which appeared in the *South Carolina Gazette*, was fake news. It pressed several emotional buttons to increase support for armed resistance. The author, probably Peter Timothy, called on the people to "adopt immediate measures for defense. The choice is simple: abject submission or noble resistance. Your freedom, the virtue of your women, the blood of your guiltless children, may be the price of a few days' delay."

It is significant that Dealey and Martin were Roman Catholic. Their neighbors may not have known that before the confrontation with Hubart. The practice of Catholicism was illegal in colonial South Carolina, and they may have kept their religion secret prior to this time. It is difficult to understand why they thought the Protestant government of Britain was about to improve the situation of Catholics. Parliament had enacted severe penal laws against the practice of Catholicism, especially in Ireland. A recent act of Parliament probably accounted for their optimism: the Quebec Act. Most colonists knew about it, and it frightened and angered them. One of the act's provisions allowed the free practice of the Roman Catholic faith in Quebec. Another removed any reference to the Protestant faith from the oath of allegiance to Great Britain. The act was designed to reassure the overwhelmingly French Catholic population of Quebec, who had only recently (1763) become British subjects. Nervous colonists to the south feared it was part of a British plot to enlist French Canadians to force tyranny and perhaps even Catholicism on them. Preposterous? Yes, but timing can be everything. In the summer of 1775 and on into the next year, paranoia ran deep in the thirteen colonies. Reason often took a back seat to conspiracy theories. Many colonists believed rumors that Britain's government had been infiltrated with papist authoritarians as well as treasonous Scots. Some Whigs encouraged and exploited such beliefs to unite the colonies against British rule. The South Carolina Constitution of 1776 and the American Declaration of Independence both list the Quebec Act as among the colonial grievances that led to revolution. Ironically, during the War for Independence, the new United States allied with Catholic, absolutist France and Spain against Protestant Britain.

After hearing Hubart's tale, the council directed the Sons of Liberty to arrange an appropriate punishment. They seized Dealey and Martin and dragged them to the State House at Broad and Meeting. There they assembled an extralegal "citizens' court" to try the offenders. Based on Hubart's testimony, the "jurors" found them guilty of obnoxious behavior. For this crime, the kangaroo court sentenced them to be dressed in "An American Suit of Clothing," a euphemism for tarring and feathering. The enforcers removed the offenders' upper clothing, poured hot tar over their bare skin and then dropped the feathers on the sticky tar. The procedure was humiliating, painful and dangerous. Hot tar could cause severe burns and other injuries, even death. After they were suitably attired, the mob tossed them in a cart and paraded them about town, ending at a wharf on Bay Street. A boat, appropriately named *Liberty*, waited there to take them to a ship anchored in Rebellion Road. Their final punishment was to be banished to Britain. Dealey accepted his fate. Martin begged to be allowed to remain in Charleston to take care of his family. He promised never to repeat his offensive behavior. The Whigs allowed him to stay after he agreed to write a public apology.

On August 11, the Liberty Boys repeated the lesson on the body of a British gunner from Fort Johnson, Sergeant George Walker. A ship captain claimed that Sergeant Walker had refused to toast "damnation to King George" and declared he would "drink damnation to rebels instead." The Liberty Boys seized Walker and assembled a "jury" of locals. They sentenced Walker to be dressed in a new suit of clothing, "without the assistance of a single tailor," as Arthur Middleton put it. Once the mob had clothed Walker in tar and feathers, they put him in a donkey cart and dragged him around town. Middleton called it a "circumcartation." The crowd pelted Walker with stones and filth along the way. The parade route took them past the houses and shops of royal officials and other "non-Associators." At each stop, they forced Walker to drink damnation

*Tarring and Feathering* by Philip Dawe, 1774. *John Carter Brown Library.*

to the residents. As the mob carted him about, they came upon Milligen. It was a stiflingly hot August day. He was sitting on the porch of his mother-in-law's house. The crowd charged toward him, shouting that he should join Walker in the cart, that he was the "greater villain." Milligen claimed that hundreds of "snakes" immediately surrounded him, "hissing and threatening and abusing me." Milligen's wife came outside. When she saw what was happening, she fainted. He carried her back inside. Some of the crowd poured into the house, "and almost horrified to death my mother-in-law, who is near eighty years of age." He decided to get the mob out of her house by going to his own close by. He carried his wife through the crowd. They let the couple go but followed them, continuing to threaten him. After he got his wife into the house, he and a Black servant managed to force the rabble out and lock the gate. With evening coming on, the crowd dispersed. They washed Walker off and dumped him in the harbor. He might have drowned if sailors from a nearby British ship had not rescued him. Walker sustained severe burns and damage to an eye. Timothy called the incident "a decent tarring" and a salutary lesson: "I believe there was scarce a non-subscriber who did not tremble." Milligen believed the attack on him was orchestrated. It may have been. Middleton wrote that Milligen had told a messenger from the council that he would not sign the Association and might not obey a summons from that body. Middleton noted that Milligen had said this before "the show of yesterday; whether that will alter his tone or no, I cannot say."

The next day, several friends of Milligen came to his house and urged him to leave the colony immediately for his safety. They told him he had become obnoxious to the Council of Safety because he had treated them with disrespect. One of his visitors was a member of the council who told Milligen that if he stayed the best treatment he could expect was "a disgraceful and dangerous imprisonment." The royal governor, Lord William Campbell, also advised him to leave. Milligen agreed to go but only after his next scheduled meeting with the council. On the appointed day, he remained as defiant as ever. Laurens, who may have been the council member who warned Milligen, was not there. Charles Pinckney was in the chair, but Arthur Middleton took the lead in questioning Milligen. He asked Milligen to sign an oath that he would not oppose the actions of the Provincial Congress. Milligen refused. Middleton asked him if he understood the possible consequences of his refusal. "I do," Milligen replied. "I have observed the justice meted out by liberty mobs." Middleton snapped. Those were justified actions of the people, he said, not a mob.

The council dismissed Milligen. As he left, Middleton advised him to "be careful of your attire" and remember to take his kilt along. Milligen left, followed by laughter. Once outside, he jumped into a waiting carriage. It raced to a nearby wharf, where a naval skiff waited to take him to safety aboard a British sloop anchored in the harbor, HMS *Tamar*. Middleton wrote to Drayton that Milligen had run off because he longed to become a great man and had now begun his "career of glory." Middleton suggested that another reason for Milligen's departure was "an unconquerable dislike to the mode of clothing lately adopted....[He] by no means wished to be exalted in this damned hot country; but would rather have a high place in Scotland."

Governor Campbell had organized Milligen's escape. He arranged for Milligen to take a mail packet to England and report on the situation in South Carolina. Milligen compiled a report during the voyage. He arrived in London and delivered it to Lord Dartmouth, secretary of state for the colonies. Milligen characterized the Carolina rebels as pampered grumblers who lived in one of the most prosperous corners of the empire. He accused them of using lies, threats and violence to achieve their "wicked" ends. They forced people to sign the Association to protect themselves by "making all who subscribed as guilty as themselves." They hoped to escape punishment by hiding "amongst a multitude of sinners." Many of the people who signed the Association, he claimed, did so under threats of economic ruin and physical intimidation. The gullible were frightened into signing by false rumors of British-inspired slave rebellions and Indian attacks. The Whigs had exploited "the bugbear of instigated insurrections" to create an army "to protect themselves, and to intimidate and distress His Majesty's loyal subjects." Many White Charlestonians had swallowed the fabrications. They reacted as if they were possessed by a demon, he wrote. Stories flew about that the slaves on this or that plantation had killed their masters and run off into the woods with guns. The Provincial Congress advised citizens to bring their guns to church on Sundays to prevent a surprise attack. They ordered Whites to perform patrol duty to prevent the movement and meetings of Blacks. When no uprising occurred, Milligen charged, people began to doubt the stories. The Whigs responded by arresting and interrogating several "suspicious" people. They announced that they had uncovered proof the British were trying to instigate a slave revolt and executed the alleged plot leader, Thomas Jeremiah.

Milligen's analysis was largely correct. The popular reaction to the rumors of slave revolts and Indian attacks is one of the key things that divided

Whites into Whigs and Loyalists in the summer of 1775. What the British government did at that point was less important than what people believed it capable of doing. It is not surprising that many Whites denounced a government they believed "was promising every Negro that would murder his Master and family that he should have his Master's plantation" and was willing to approve "the most horrible butcheries of innocent women and children." What seems more surprising is that some people continued to support such a diabolical government. To remain loyal required one to believe that the Whigs were peddling fake news. Milligen held that belief. It is difficult to know how many others in Charleston shared his views. Few Loyalists were as outspoken as he in the summer of 1775. After delivering his report to the government in London, Milligen went to Scotland. He never returned to Charleston, his home for more than twenty years. In later life, he changed his surname to Milligen-Johnston in honor of his mother, the last of her family line. He died in Dumfries in 1799. He did not gain "a high place" in Scotland.

# WILLIAM WRAGG

In the south choir aisle of Westminster Abbey in London there lies a memorial in marble to a wealthy South Carolina planter. His name was William Wragg. He drowned off the coast of Holland in September 1777. Wragg's sister had the monument erected in 1779. The inscription describes his tragic fate and, as monuments to people generally do, praises his character: "In him, strong natural parts, improved by education, together with love of justice and humanity, formed the valuable character of a good man." Like Drayton and Middleton, Wragg was a prominent member of the Lowcountry elite, owner of plantations and hundreds of slaves. Unlike them, he was a staunch Loyalist. The monument to Wragg is the only one in the abbey dedicated to an American-born participant in the War for Independence. Westminster Abbey is famed for containing remains and monuments memorializing British monarchs, military heroes and cultural icons. Two British army officers who served during the Revolutionary War are interred there. One is Major John André, who Americans hanged as a spy in 1780. The other, General John Burgoyne, is best known for losing the pivotal Battle of Saratoga in upstate New York in 1777. Unlike them, Wragg did not fight in the War for Independence.

Wragg was born in Charleston in 1714 to merchant Samuel Wragg and Marie Dubose. Shortly after William's birth, Samuel purchased a large plantation, Ashley Barony. At age four, William experienced a harrowing encounter with legendary pirate Edward Teach, also known as Blackbeard. Samuel had taken William along on a coastal trading voyage in May 1718 when Blackbeard captured their ship, the *Crowley*. Teach crammed all eighty of the *Crowley*'s passengers and crew into the hold of his flagship, the *Queen Anne's Revenge*. He held them hostage to a demand for an unusual ransom—not money, gold or spoils, but medicines. His battered crew were suffering from disease and wounds. Teach sent one of the hostages to Charleston to deliver his demand. After several days, no medicines arrived. Teach threatened to kill Samuel and loot Charleston if the town did not meet his demand. The city authorities finally sent a large consignment of medicines. Blackbeard put the hostages ashore, but not before stripping them of most of their clothing. They had to walk a long distance through the woods to town. Later that year, a pirate-hunting expedition cornered and killed Blackbeard off the coast of North Carolina.

*William Wragg* by Jeremiah Theus, circa 1750. *Detroit Institute of Arts*.

Having survived his pirate encounter, young William embarked on another adventure several years later. His parents sent him to England to be educated. He attended Westminster School, Oxford University and the Middle Temple, where he studied law. He was admitted to the English bar in 1733 at age nineteen and practiced law in England until about 1750. His father died that year, and he returned to South Carolina. He inherited a fortune: several plantations and more than 250 enslaved laborers. Like many elite planters, he entered politics. In 1753, the Crown appointed him to the governor's council.

Perhaps because he had spent so many years in England, Wragg was a strong advocate of the prerogatives of the council and the royal governors against the pretensions of the Commons House of Assembly. He was so outspoken that Governor Lyttleton removed him from the council in 1757 to appease the assembly. Wragg was elected to the assembly the next year. There, he disputed the claims of colonial autonomy being put forward by Christopher Gadsden. He accused Gadsden of having lost his reason and of putting his own interests ahead of those of South Carolina. Wragg opposed the creation of the Stamp Act Congress and the Non-Importation Movement. In 1768, he resigned from the assembly, he said, due to his inability to stem its increasing opposition to British rule. He never sought political office again. The government in London offered him jobs in the colonial administration, but he refused them, declaring that he did not want to profit from his loyalty.

Like Milligen, Wragg refused to sign the Association. The Council of Safety summoned him to explain why he would not. He replied, "I'd despise myself if I subscribed to an opinion contrary to the dictates of my conscience. I have no hostile intentions toward you gentlemen, but I believe the logical outcome of your current measures will be an attempt to separate from the mother country." Henry Laurens, in the chair, denied that they had any such plan. The council would leave him alone if he signed the Association. In response to this barely veiled threat, Wragg asked, "What kind of supporter would I be if I signed this document under duress?" The council ordered Wragg confined to his plantation, essentially putting him under house arrest. He agreed to abide by the Council of Safety's decision but mocked their fears of "the formidable power of twenty gentlemen whose age, disposition, and education of most of them hardly qualify them as dangerous conspirators." He was referring mainly to holders of Crown offices in Charleston. In 1777, the Whigs banished Wragg after he refused to sign an oath of allegiance to the new state of South Carolina. Leaving behind his wife and daughters, he boarded a ship bound for Amsterdam, taking his son, Billy, and Tom, an enslaved servant. The ship sank in a storm off the coast of the Netherlands. Wragg drowned trying to save his son, but Tom managed to rescue Billy. The Westminster memorial depicts the boys clinging to a piece of wreckage with the sinking vessel behind them. His fellow Loyalist George Milligen wrote of Wragg that "he would have been an ornament to Sparta or Rome in their most virtuous days."

# THOMAS JEREMIAH

For Charleston, 1775 was a year of frightening rumors. The most terrifying was the Whig claim that the British were inciting slave rebellions. Whigs were simultaneously accusing the British government of threatening American liberty. The hypocrisy of slaveholders crying liberty in danger did not go unnoticed in Britain or America. The English writer and lexicographer Samuel Johnson pounced on it immediately. In January 1775, he published "Taxation No Tyranny," an essay on the dispute between Britain and the thirteen colonies. In it, Johnson asked, "How is it that we hear the loudest yelps for liberty from the drivers of Negroes?" Rebellious colonists brushed aside Johnson's rather weak arguments about taxation and representation. His remarks about their inconsistency regarding liberty and slavery stung. Johnson hated slavery. He once toasted "the next slave rebellion in Jamaica." In 1752, he adopted Samuel Barber, a young man who had been enslaved. He freed and educated Barber at his own expense and made him residual beneficiary in his will.

The fear of slave rebellion easily aroused panic in South Carolina, the only American colony where Blacks outnumbered Whites. In some Lowcountry parishes, the ratio was as high as four or five to one. Memories of the Stono Rebellion of 1739, when slaves killed twenty-five Whites, ran deep. Fears of a slave revolt were never far from the minds of Lowcountry Whites. They intensified during the conflict between Britain and its colonies. Henry Laurens articulated the fear. During the Stamp Act Crisis of the 1760s, he noted that some "negroes" had imitated White cries for liberty. This "peculiar incident," Laurens wrote, "revealed in what dread the citizens lived among the black savages." Near the end of 1774, a Black Methodist preacher, David Margate, arrived in Charleston. Margate was accused of preaching that God would liberate the slaves as he had freed the Hebrews from Egyptian bondage. His White sponsors rushed him away to save him from a mob. In February 1775, the Charleston Grand Jury accused Peter Hinds of allowing "Negro Preachers" to come to his house and grounds, where they delivered "dangerous and subversive" sermons to gatherings of slaves. The dangerous ideas they were spreading no doubt included stories that Britain was going to liberate the slaves. Virginia's governor Lord Dunmore had already threatened to free and arm slaves to defend Crown authority. Anxiety reached fever pitch in the summer of 1775. South Carolina's Provincial Congress appointed a committee of five to investigate rumors of an impending slave revolt. In mid-June, they reported that a free Black man was plotting a slave revolt to help the British. Thomas Jeremiah was one of about five hundred free Blacks in the colony. He owned a fishing business and worked as a harbor pilot, guiding ships through the treacherous bar at the entrance of Charleston Harbor. He was possibly the wealthiest free Black in Charleston, with an estate worth close to £1,000. Whites usually called him "Jerry," from reluctance to accord him the respect of his full name.

The case against Jeremiah rested primarily on the testimony of two slaves, Jemmy and Sambo. A slave patrol arrested them on the road leading out of Charleston. Their captors said they were acting suspiciously and carried no passes. Both worked about the wharves and on coastal schooners. The patrol took them to the Sugar House, a building used to incarcerate and punish "problem" slaves. The authorities subjected Jemmy and Sambo to "rigorous" interrogation. They confessed that Jeremiah had recruited them to support a slave revolt on behalf of the British, who were coming to help "the poor Negroes." He told them that he was collecting gunpowder and guns but needed more. He boasted that he was going to set fire to Charleston and that if a British fleet arrived, he would pilot them across the bar into the harbor. How much of this was true, how much derived from leading questions by threatening inquisitors and how much was invention we will probably never know. The authorities charged Jemmy as a co-conspirator. They convinced him that the only way he could save himself was to incriminate Jeremiah, which he did.

In his report to Lord Dartmouth, George Milligen called Jeremiah's trial illegal. It was certainly a mockery of the English judicial system. The Provisional Government tried him under the Negro Act of 1740, enacted in response to the Stono Rebellion of 1739. Without the benefit of a lawyer, a tribunal of two justices of the peace and five White men acted as prosecution, judge and jury. Milligen argued that Jeremiah should have been tried by a jury because he was free, propertied and a Christian. The testimony of his accusers should have been inadmissible because they were neither free nor Christian. The Negro Act tribunal found him guilty and sentenced him to death by hanging and burning. As an act of "humanity," they added that he should be hanged until dead before being burned. The evidence against Jeremiah was conflicting and flimsy. The testimony of Sambo and Jemmy was suspect. After the sentencing, Jemmy retracted his testimony in a conversation with Reverend Robert Smith. The Provisional Government refused to consider his retraction. Jeremiah proclaimed his innocence to the last. On August 18, 1775, the sentence of execution was carried out on the green across from the Sugar House.

We may never know if Jeremiah was trying to organize a slave rebellion or if the Whigs had manufactured the plot to stoke White anger against the British government. Milligen argued the Whigs had framed Jeremiah to sway Charlestonians into supporting their resort to arms. "Thus, this poor fellow fell a victim to the groundless fears of some, and the wicked policy of others." He called the execution a judicial murder. Jeremiah was an appealing candidate for sacrificial lamb. His wealth, skills and prominence made him a living reproach to White claims that Africans were fit for nothing but slave labor. A sharp tongue may have contributed to his undoing. On a previous occasion, officials sentenced him to a day in the stocks for insulting a ship captain. Henry Laurens thought that humiliating and painful experience gave Jeremiah a motive for revenge. Jeremiah's skills also worked against him. Milligen claimed that "his real crime was to be a good harbor pilot." The Whigs feared "Jerry" might guide an attacking British fleet into Charleston Harbor. The fear was not groundless, but eliminating Jeremiah did not exorcize it. Other Black pilots knew the harbor well. One of them, Sampson, guided the British fleet during its attack on Sullivan's Island in June 1776 and later piloted other British ships along the South Atlantic coast. Peter Timothy commented that Sampson ought to be hanged as an example to others. Jeremiah was a skilled volunteer firefighter. His accusers used that against him as well, claiming that he was probably starting fires to exhibit his skills. That was the view of Charleston's fire master, Daniel Cannon, who sat on the tribunal that tried Jeremiah. One of the charges against Jeremiah was that he planned to set fire to Charleston when the British arrived. Jeremiah's alleged slave plot pushed anxious Whites toward the conclusion that they must sever ties with a government capable of such wickedness. Other events were pushing them in that direction, including rumors about Lord William Campbell, the new royal governor, who arrived when fears of a slave revolt were at their height.

# SARAH IZARD AND LORD WILLIAM CAMPBELL

Loyalists came from many different backgrounds. They chose loyalism for a variety of reasons. Some held offices or jobs under the British government and had taken oaths of allegiance to the Crown. Others had received land or mercantile privileges from the Crown and feared losing them if they supported rebellion. Thousands of enslaved persons became Loyalists because the British offered them freedom in return for their help. Many Native Americans supported the British government because it had tried to restrict the movement of White settlers onto their lands. Sarah Izard became a Loyalist through marriage. The revolution forced her to choose between her husband and her family and friends. Sarah was born in South Carolina around 1745, the daughter of Ralph and Rebecca Izard. Online genealogy sources about Sarah and her family are conflicting and confusing, sometimes hilarious. Some sites put her mother's age as nine when she gave birth to Sarah. Others claim that Sarah's parents were Ralph and Alice Delancey Izard, who were born in the same decade as she was. Some claim that the same Ralph Izard, who became an American senator and diplomat, was her brother. He was in fact her cousin. To add to the confusion, she did have a brother named Ralph Izard, but not the Ralph Izard who became a senator.

Sarah was in her late teens when she met a Royal Navy captain, Lord William Campbell. He had come to Charleston in 1762 as commander of the frigate HMS *Nightingale*. He was the fourth son of Scotland's most powerful aristocrat, the Duke of Argyll. Charlestonians welcomed him as their defender. The Seven Years' War was nearly over and Britain was winning decisively. It was officially over by the time the pair married in April 1763, making Sarah Lady William Campbell. Their wedding was a major event for the local elite. The notice in the *South Carolina Gazette* mentions that Sarah was "a young lady esteemed one of the most considerable fortunes in the province." Translation: she was a fine catch for the fourth son of a duke unlikely to inherit much wealth. The younger son of a duke was also a good catch for the daughter of a provincial planter, a prestigious link to the British aristocracy. With peace restored, the Royal Navy recalled Lord William to Britain in 1764. Sarah thus entered the London social whirl. Joshua Reynolds painted her portrait with one of her beloved whippets. Lord William served a term in Parliament as MP for his family's seat in Argyllshire. In 1766, the Crown appointed him royal governor of Nova Scotia. It was not exactly a plum job. Nova Scotia was cold, poor and sparsely populated, a huge change from London. Seven years later, a more attractive position became available. In 1773, the British government recalled the royal governor of South Carolina, Lord Charles Montagu. Lord William lobbied for the vacancy. Sarah must have been delighted at the prospect of returning home. Family influence helped Lord William to secure the job. Before heading for South Carolina, William and Sarah returned to Britain. They did not get to Charleston until June 18, 1775. To say they arrived at an inopportune time would be an understatement. The situation in South Carolina had altered so drastically in the previous months as to catch them, and the British government, unprepared. At the time William and Sarah arrived, the government's ministers believed that their colonial problem was confined to Massachusetts or perhaps New England. They looked on South Carolina as grumpy but not rebellious. They were confident enough of its fundamental loyalty to send a surveying ship on a scientific mission to chart Charleston Harbor. One reason for the government's confidence was the demographic reality. In a province where enslaved Blacks outnumbered Whites, they reasoned, it would be lunacy for disgruntled colonists to embark on a military confrontation with the empire. William and Sarah had no idea how fundamentally the political situation had changed since they left Britain. They were in for a severe shock.

From the outset, most local leaders refused to cooperate with the new governor or treat him as anything but suspicious. Some Whigs wanted to prevent him from landing in the first place. Charleston was awash with rumors of perfidious British plots to subdue the colonies. One of them related to the arrival of Lord William himself. It came in a letter from Arthur Lee,

*Left*: Sarah Izard Campbell (Lady William Campbell), by Nalan Laluk. *Copy of portrait by Charles Fraser in Gibbes Museum of Art, based on original portrait by Joshua Reynolds.*

*Right*: Lord William Campbell, attributed to Richard Cosway, circa 1760s. *Argyll Estates, by kind permission of His Grace, the Duke of Argyll.*

a colonial representative in London. Lee claimed to have intelligence that HMS *Scorpion*, the sloop bringing the governor to Charleston, was carrying thousands of guns to distribute to Loyalists, slaves and "savages." The intelligence was false. The most dangerous weapons on board were probably Sarah's whippet hounds. Whigs spread news of Lee's letter through the city, inflaming an already volatile situation and priming the citizens to view the governor's arrival with profound distrust.

Charlestonians had greeted the previous governor, Lord Charles Montagu, with the ringing of church bells, large cheering crowds, saluting cannonades and a sumptuous dinner at Dillon's Tavern. On this occasion, there were no bells, crowds, cheers or dinner. The waterfront was nearly deserted as *Scorpion* docked at a wharf near the Exchange. A detachment of blue-coated soldiers stood ready to escort the lord and his lady, but whether as dignitaries or prisoners was unclear. A few royal officials came out to greet them but none of the leading gentlemen of the town. Even the lieutenant governor, William Bull, was absent. Unable to control the situation, and with friends and family on both sides, Bull had retreated to his Ashley Hall plantation. One wonders what went through the minds of William and Sarah as they observed this forlorn and frosty welcome. Sarah had brought their three children from England. She must have been feeling extremely anxious. After ten years away, this was not the homecoming she had expected. The soldiers escorted the Campbells to the mansion of merchant Miles Brewton on King Street, a magnificent Georgian edifice built from profits amassed from the slave trade. Brewton's wife was Sarah's cousin Mary. The Brewtons had agreed to entertain Lord and Lady William for a few days while the governor's mansion at 34 Meeting Street was being prepared for them. Sarah soon learned that most of her family and friends opposed the government her husband represented. That evening, Lord William received another brutal reminder of his predicament. He was walking about the neighborhood with his secretary, Alexander Innes, when they came to an artillery post at the State House at Broad and Meeting Streets. A soldier stopped them, claiming he had orders from Congress not to let anyone pass. Innes told the soldier that he was speaking to the governor. "I've been ordered not to acknowledge the governor," the soldier replied. The next day, William Henry Drayton led a Whig deputation to meet Lord William. Drayton harangued Campbell on the wickedness of the British government and defended the actions of the Provincial Congress. He ended by proclaiming, "We prefer death to slavery." The governor replied that he had come on a mission of peace. But, he added, he could not recognize the authority of the Provincial Congress, only that of the constitutional Commons House of Assembly. He convened the Commons House to find that the members treated the institution with contempt. They met each day and promptly adjourned, then reconvened a short distance away, as the Provincial Congress. In that extralegal body, which was already the functional government, they conducted business free of Lord William's interference. Lacking military support, Campbell was reduced to futile protest.

The execution of Thomas Jeremiah a few weeks later convinced Campbell of his utter powerlessness. He labeled Jeremiah's trial a gross miscarriage of justice. Jeremiah's offense, if any, was restricted to speech, not action, and should not have carried the death penalty. The trial was illegal and the evidence against the accused exceedingly weak and suspect. Jeremiah was "the victim of the accursed politics of this country." Campbell tried to pardon Jeremiah using his executive power, only to discover he had no power. He appealed to the president of the Provincial Congress and the Council of Safety, Henry Laurens, requesting him to press for a review of the case. Laurens responded that Jeremiah had received a fair trial and that the Congress and council refused to intervene. After Jeremiah's execution, Campbell wrote an anguished letter to Lord Dartmouth. "I could not save him My Lord! The very reflection harrows my soul....My blood run cold when I read on what grounds they had doomed a fellow creature to death." The execution was judicial murder and Jeremiah's executioners "a set of barbarians who are worse than the most cruel savages any history has described." Campbell's intervention in the Jeremiah case infuriated the Whigs. Peter Timothy wrote to Drayton in the backcountry, that "more force was exerted to save [Jeremiah] than there would have been for you or me—unless for our exaltation [hanging]." The word *force* here is interesting, considering Campbell had no force and the Whigs threatened to use force against him. A liberty mob surrounded his house on Meeting Street and accused him of being involved in the slave insurrection plot. They threatened to erect gallows outside his house, drag him out into the street and force him to hang Jeremiah himself.

Events now moved swiftly toward the end of even a nominal royal administration. A few weeks after the execution, the council discovered that Campbell was in contact with backcountry Loyalists, urging them to be ready to fight for the king. In early September, he met secretly with Moses Kirkland, who had sneaked into Charleston under cover of darkness. To the Whigs, Kirkland was a traitor. He had joined them, only to change sides when they failed to give him the military command he desired. The Whigs learned of the meeting when they captured one of Kirkland's companions on his way out of town. Campbell's encouragement of backcountry Loyalists produced the worst of both worlds. It mobilized Whig fury and did nothing to help the Loyalists. They wanted leadership and an assurance of British military assistance. Campbell had nothing to offer but the king's gratitude and his belief that British ships and soldiers would soon arrive. A motion in the Provincial Congress to authorize Campbell's arrest failed by a slim majority. Convinced that his presence was useless and his life in danger, he dissolved the assembly and fled. On the night of September 15, he boarded a small boat moored behind his residence at 34 Meeting Street. The boat took him down Vanderhorst Creek and out to HMS *Tamar*, anchored at Rebellion Roads. Historians traditionally date the end of royal rule in South Carolina to Campbell's flight. In truth, royal rule had ended in all but name months before he arrived in Charleston. On the same day as he fled the city, Whig soldiers seized Fort Johnson, only to find he had ordered it abandoned.

Lady Campbell remained in Charleston at first. About two weeks later, she applied to the Council of Safety for permission to join her husband. The

Whig leaders initially prevented her. They were trying to persuade Lord William to return to the city, in a confused effort to pretend that the royal connection had not been severed. Laurens wrote to Sarah on September 29 that "nothing but the expectation of seeing his lordship in Charles Town tomorrow has prevented their giving such orders as would have secured your ladyship a safe passage to the *Tamar* without hindrance or trouble." Laurens added that if the governor declined the invitation to return, he would apply for an order allowing her to join him. Campbell refused to return while the province was in a state of open rebellion. Around that time, he fell ill of a fever. Laurens gave Sarah a pass permitting her to go see him and to take Dr. Alexander Garden along to treat his illness. Afterward, she returned to town, but Whig harassment led her to flee Charleston one night a few weeks later. A Black fisherman who had been covertly ferrying supplies to the British ships took her to her husband in his boat.

Lord William may have left Charleston, but he remained just off stage, commanding three small British ships moored near the entrance to Charleston harbor. In addition to *Tamar*, he had commandeered two other vessels that had recently arrived. One was a mail packet, the *Swallow*. The other was a surveying ship, *Cherokee*. The survey leader, Dutch cartographer William Gerard De Brahm, was angry when he learned he could not proceed with his mission. Campbell's secretary, Alexander Innes, complained that De Brahm plagued them with his demands. The Dutchman didn't understand the gravity of the situation, Innes wrote, adding that it was "a fine time to talk of his surveys of a country" when its possession was in dispute.

The Council of Safety viewed Campbell's flotilla as a danger to Charleston. None of Lord William's ships possessed much firepower, but they were the only armed ships in the harbor. Hoping to prevent what was happening in Virginia, the council agreed to provide food and supplies to the British ships. To keep them on a short leash, the council prohibited anyone from carrying supplies to them without its approval. Concern about Lord William's ships led the council to approve Drayton's proposal to create a South Carolina navy. The first vessel was a converted merchant schooner, the *Defense*. On November 11, it exchanged fire with *Tamar* and *Cherokee* in the nearly forgotten Battle of Hog Island. Drayton was aboard *Defense* as it towed the hulks of four old schooners out toward the island. Its mission was to sink the hulks in Hog Island Channel to block the channel. The aim was to force ships approaching Charleston to pass under the guns at Fort Johnson on James Island. As *Defense* neared the channel, the British ships fired on it. The vessels exchanged shots for several hours. The gunnery on both sides was poor. None of the ships took a major hit and no one was hurt. Before darkness ended the engagement, the crew of the *Defense* managed to sink three hulks. They sank two more on November 24, effectively blocking the channel. Not long after, the British squadron was reinforced by the arrival of the sloop that had brought Lord and Lady William to Charleston, the *Scorpion*.

In the meantime, Campbell created another reason for Whig alarm. He landed some of his sailors on Sullivan's Island. They were joined there by runaway slaves who decided that the British were the only ones who might help them secure their freedom. In early November, Limus, one of Joshua Eden's slaves, told him Eden "he will be free, that he will serve no man, and that he will be conquered or governed by no man." Limus ran away, probably to join the runaways on Sullivan's Island. The advertisement offering a reward for his recapture mentioned that "he has had the ends of three fingers cut off" and was "well known in Charleston for his saucy and impudent tongue." The Whigs knew that Virginia's royal governor, Lord Dunmore, had fled to a ship off the coast, near Norfolk. His presence there had attracted runaways who were allegedly terrorizing the local White population. Dunmore followed with a proclamation offering freedom to slaves who rallied to the king's support. Charleston newspapers suppressed the story, but it spread among the enslaved population anyway. More of them flocked to Sullivan's Island. A false newspaper report that Dunmore was selling runaways into slavery in the West Indies also failed to stem the exodus. By the end of November, the number of runaways on the island had swollen to almost five hundred.

Lord William did not issue a Dunmore-style proclamation. But he welcomed the runaways and employed them against the rebels. Bands of sailors, runaways and a few White Loyalists conducted raids on plantations in nearby Christ Church Parish to secure food and supplies. The Whigs feared that the island might become the center of a slave rebellion. They concluded that the actions of Dunmore and Campbell were part of a wicked plan to terrorize the White population. With no sense of irony, George Washington denounced Dunmore as an "arch traitor to the rights of humanity." John Rutledge declared "humanity must revolt" against a government scheming to "make ignorant domestics subservient to the most wicked purposes." The Council of Safety decided it had to remove what Henry Laurens called "this alarming evil" from Sullivan's Island. Just before Christmas, they sent a force of two hundred Whig Rangers to disperse the runaways. Disguised as Indians, they attacked shortly before dawn, achieving complete surprise.

They killed dozens of the runaways and captured others, along with a few Whites. They destroyed the island's pesthouse, where in "normal" times newly arrived Africans underwent quarantine prior to being brought into town for sale. On this occasion, the building was serving as a shelter for the runaways. Some of them managed to escape to the British ships or to Morris Island across the harbor. The Whigs occupied Sullivan's Island and declared they would no longer supply the British ships with provisions. With his position untenable, Campbell withdrew to the British stronghold at St. Augustine in Florida. From there, he and Sarah sailed to Britain. Sarah never returned to her native land. Campbell would come back for one more brief appearance.

The Whigs expected a British attack on Charleston that winter. The fear produced an exodus from the city. Most White women and many men fled to the country, taking their children and valuables. Henry Laurens wrote to his son John that he was busy moving possessions from his house in town to his plantation at Mepkin. A bit overdramatically, he claimed to be "sitting in a house stripped of its furniture and in danger of being knocked down in a very few days by a cannon ball." Known Loyalists were forced to leave, for fear they would aid an attacking British force. Men who had volunteered to defend South Carolina streamed in from the country. Their officers, mostly Lowcountry aristocrats, struggled to shape raw recruits into an organized and orderly force. Doing so required limiting the liberty the volunteers were supposedly fighting for. Months of waiting for an expected British attack gave the officers, themselves often inexperienced, time to try to train their men. It also created problems. The men had enlisted to fight. Instead, they had to drill, obey and combat boredom. Many of them sought to escape the monotony in the city's taverns and brothels. Colonel Charles Cotesworth Pinckney complained of drunkenness, theft and desertion among his men. Some of the enlistees were quartered in houses left vacant by those fleeing inland. To keep warm in winter, they broke up and burned much of the furniture that remained.

The early months of 1776 passed nervously but peacefully. War came to Charleston in earnest at the end of May. Lord William Campbell returned, accompanied by a British fleet and army. A former naval officer, he served on HMS *Bristol*, flagship of Admiral Sir Peter Parker. The fleet carried about three thousand British soldiers under the command of General Henry Clinton. Charleston was not their initial objective. General William Howe, British commander in North America, sent them south to aid Loyalists in eastern North Carolina. When they arrived in Wilmington, they discovered that a Whig force had routed and dispersed the Loyalists at Moore's Creek Bridge. There was no longer any force to aid. Parker and Clinton decided to attack Charleston instead. After they arrived off the South Carolina coast, a combination of indecision and bad weather delayed their attack nearly a month. Their plan was ill-conceived and poorly executed. A quick and direct assault on Charleston could have made things difficult for the defenders. Instead, they focused on recapturing Sullivan's Island, where the Whigs were scrambling to finish a new harbor fortification. Drayton designed the fort. Housebuilder Daniel Cannon supervised the work. The fort, made of palmetto logs, was constructed by Charleston artisans and slaves commandeered to do the heavy labor.

Clinton landed his soldiers on Long Island (now the Isle of Palms). The British plan called for them to wade across Breach Inlet, the narrow channel separating Long and Sullivan's Islands. Due to poor reconnaissance, Clinton learned too late that the channel was too deep and the current too strong for that to be feasible. The recently arrived commander of Continental forces in the South, General Charles Lee, placed another obstacle in Clinton's way. He placed nearly eight hundred rangers on the other side of the inlet, ready to repel a British attempt to cross it in boats. On June 28, Parker's fleet attacked Fort Sullivan. Clinton's army was stranded and played no part in the battle. The fort's rubbery palmetto log walls famously withstood a furious cannonade with little damage and few casualties. In contrast, the fort's artillery inflicted severe damage on several British ships. An adverse wind blew three frigates aground on the infamous bar. Two managed to get off at high tide, but one, *Actaeon*, was abandoned and burned. Fort Sullivan's defenders were plucky and lucky. Had the British ships got past the bar, they would have been able to fire directly at the unfinished part of the fort, forcing its abandonment. The Battle of Sullivan's Island was the first major American victory of the war. For the British, who had several hundred men killed and wounded, it was a major disaster. The wounded included Parker and Campbell. During the battle, a flying splinter of wood lodged in Parker's leg, allegedly removing his breeches, or so Whig newspapers reported with glee. Parker recovered and lived for many years. Campbell was less fortunate. He was manning one of the guns on *Bristol* when an explosion drove a large splinter into his body. He died two years later from the effects of the wound. Sarah remained in Britain, where she died in 1784, aged thirty-nine.

Lord William Campbell came to South Carolina in 1775 with a disadvantage few historians have emphasized. He was a Scot at a time when many colonists viewed Scots with suspicion. Governor Dunmore

*The Battle of Fort Moultrie* by John Blake White, 1826. *Courtesy U.S. Senate Art Collection.*

of Virginia was also a Scot. Superintendent John Stuart, who had fled Charleston after the Whigs accused him of plotting Indian attacks, was a Scot. Many American Whigs viewed all of them as agents of a Scottish conspiracy against liberty. According to this theory, which originated with English Whigs, authoritarian Scots were conspiring to gain control of the British government. Whigs like John Wilkes accused the king's former Scottish tutor, Lord Bute, of being the gray eminence behind the plot. George III had chosen Bute to be his prime minister in 1762. Bute was cultured but lacked political savvy. He was the first Scot to hold the office of prime minister, at a time when many people in England viewed Scots as barbaric, authoritarian and potentially traitorous. Only seventeen years before, an army of Scottish Highlanders had invaded England in a failed attempt to restore the Catholic Stuarts to the British throne. To add spice to the story, English Whigs claimed Bute was having an affair with the king's mother. Bute's tenure as prime minister was brief. George III removed him from office in 1763. Despite his departure, Whigs in Britain and America continued to accuse Bute of conspiring against their liberty for years. The boot (from Bute) became a common symbol of tyranny. To people on both sides of the Atlantic, even Bute's surname, Stuart, symbolized tyranny. The rights of Englishmen the

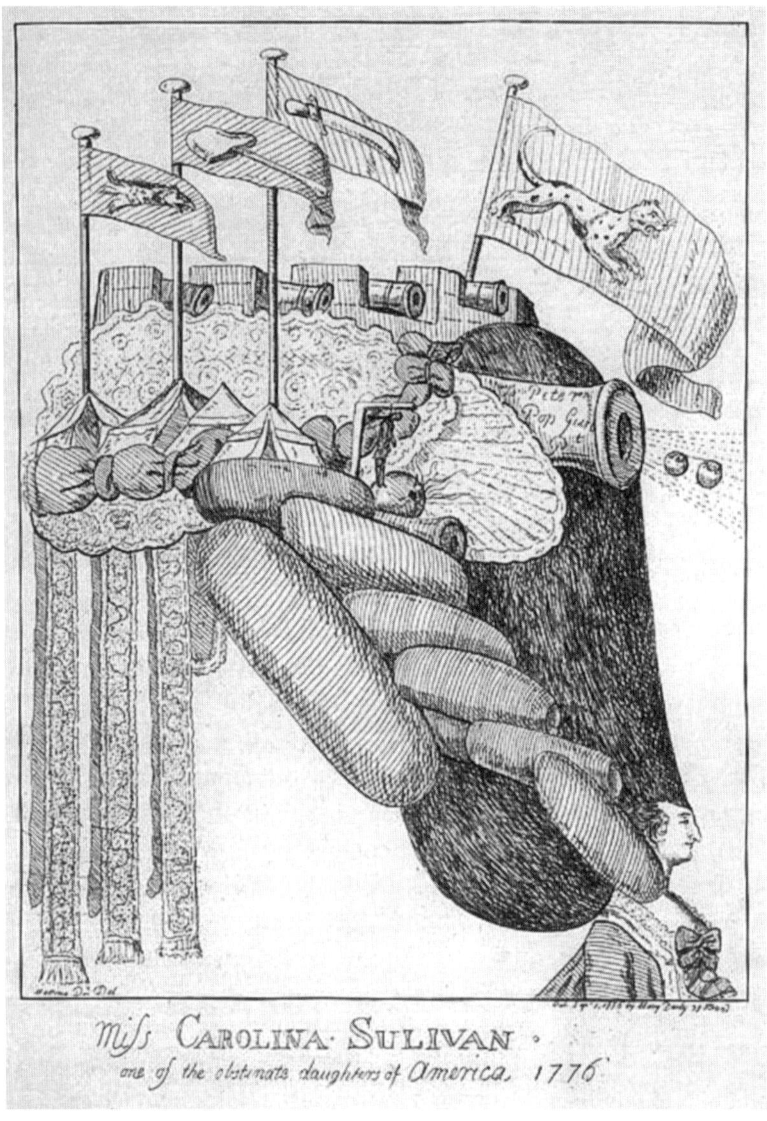


*Above*: *Miss Carolina Sulivan*, cartoon, 1776. *Library of Congress.*

*Opposite*: *Virtual Representation*, cartoon, 1775. *Library of Congress.*

colonists claimed to be defending had been secured by the so-called English Revolution of the seventeenth century. The Stuart monarchs Charles I and James II were the villains of the story.

Another Scot, William Murray, Lord Mansfield, became a favorite target of colonial Scottophobes. Mansfield was chief justice of the Court of King's Bench. In the Somerset Case (1772), he ruled that slavery had no basis in English law in precedent or statute. The Somerset ruling sent shock waves through the southern colonies. Many planters feared that Parliament might apply it to the colonies. The fear had little basis at that time. Parliament did abolish slavery in the British Empire, but not until the 1830s. In the 1770s, the antislavery movement in Britain was in its infancy. Abolitionists were beginning to have an effect on the public consciousness, but they did not have enough political influence to end the slave trade, let alone slavery in the colonies itself. Many slave-owning colonists did not understand the reality of British politics or pretended not to. They reacted hysterically to the news of the Somerset decision. Their claim that it might be applied in America led them to embrace a solution that aligned them with northern activists denying Parliament's power to tax the colonies. They denied Parliament's right to legislate at all for the colonies. In much of the south, "no taxation without representation" was not the main issue that united people against

Britain. The central issue, although never articulated directly, was "without representation, no slavery." By the early 1770s, antislavery views were spreading in the colonies as well as Britain, especially in the North. But in the interests of colonial unity, northern Whigs adopted the southern position. John Adams and Benjamin Franklin disliked slavery but argued that, like taxation, it was a domestic issue for Americans to deal with. Parliament had no right to interfere in the internal affairs of the colonies on any matter, be it taxes or slavery. The colonies had to be united to protect their sovereign rights. The issue of slavery would have to wait until that was accomplished.

In retrospect, the belief that Scots were conspiring to undermine American liberty *and* abolish American slavery seems absurd. Conspiracy theorists even accused Bute and Mansfield of being the masterminds behind the Quebec Act, as can be seen in the cartoon here. They had nothing to do with it. But to American Whigs the conspiracy theory was plausible and useful. To make way for Lord Bute, George III had removed William Pitt, whom many colonists viewed as a hero for his successful direction of the Seven Years' War and later for his opposition to the Stamp Act. Americans named many towns and streets after Pitt. Charleston erected a statue of him at the intersection of Broad and Meeting Streets. It is now located in the nearby Charleston County Judicial Center, missing an arm removed by a British cannonball in 1780.

Whig accusations of Scots political tyranny merged with resentment of Scottish competition for trade and government jobs in the colonies. The Act of Union (1707), which had merged the kingdoms of England and Scotland into the Kingdom of Great Britain, opened the colonies to Scots traders. Thousands of them took advantage of the opportunity. Scottish merchants, doctors and adventurers descended on every corner of the empire. They flocked to South Carolina and Georgia in particular. The Crown appointed Scots to many civil and military jobs in the colonies, partly as a means of keeping them loyal to the Hanoverian monarchy. The colonists were not the only ones struggling to achieve unity in the late eighteenth century. Great Britain is not much older than the United States. "British" was a new and fragile identity, less than seventy years old in 1775.

# HENRY AND JOHN LAURENS

In December 1774, Henry Laurens returned to Charleston after spending three years in Europe. The voyage was uneventful until his ship neared Charleston Harbor. A sudden storm blew it far to the south. Fighting adverse winds, the ship required two days of difficult sailing to reach the harbor entrance again. Once there, it still had to make it through the treacherous, shifting sand bar that lay at the harbor entrance. "Crossing the Bar" was fraught with danger. The obstacle had claimed more than a few lives. As luck would have it, the ship ran aground. Laurens blamed the harbor pilot, a young man who "lacked the skills of his trade." The captain panicked and was unable to act. As he stood there, moaning he would lose his ship, Laurens tried to compose him, assuring him that all was not lost, that lives were more important than property. A practical and calm appraisal of their situation could save them, he insisted. In the absence of decisive leadership, he took control of the situation. He climbed up on deck to survey the scene. The wind was blowing with gale force. High waves were pounding the ship relentlessly. They were ten miles from their goal and seven hours from daylight. Laurens gave up trying to rouse the captain, who was "wailing like a child whose toy had broke." Turning to the master and the mate, Laurens urged them to be "firm and steady." He consoled the pilot and told him to forget the accident and think how to get the ship off. Laurens went below and got two lanterns. He got the boatswain to hoist them on the ensign staff to alert vessels following them of the danger and solicit their aid. His "steadiness had a sterling effect on the crew." They worked "manfully" to extricate the ship. After a while, the rising tide moved the ship into deep water. In the morning, they took on another pilot, who brought them safely into the harbor.

In recording his actions aboard the beleaguered vessel, Laurens used words like "firm and steady," "manfully," "resolution and leadership." He compared life to a voyage in which "we must be prepared to meet all weathers," and in which "despair is useless." Looking at his words from the perspective of what awaited him in South Carolina, we could conclude that Laurens was trying to convince himself that he had leadership qualities. The storm and the bar could have been metaphors for the political crises facing the colonies. Was Laurens steeling himself to act as the captain of another vessel facing storms, the province of South Carolina? Soon after he arrived home, the First Provincial Congress convened. The delegates elected him as their president. In June, they elected him as president of the new Council of Safety. He took these positions, he wrote, in hopes of moderating the demands and actions of the radical Whigs. He soon began to sound like them. When news of the Battle of Bunker Hill arrived in July, he wrote that the outcome showed that "God is truly on our side because we fight for liberty and for virtue, and because we plead for the sacred rights of mankind." The owner of almost three hundred slaves was poised on a slippery slope.

Why did Laurens, who had not even been in South Carolina during the previous three years, rise so quickly to a position of leadership of the revolutionary party? It is true that he was one of the richest men in South Carolina. He had made a fortune from the slave trade and used the profits to buy several plantations. But wealth alone did not distinguish him. Many of the Whig leaders were wealthy. More important was Laurens's reputation as a diligent, organized businessman with a network of correspondents across the empire. That he had been in London recently gave him an insight into the British political scene He had been following events in the colonies with growing alarm. Parliament's extreme reaction to the Boston Tea Party, the Coercive Acts, helped to push him into the camp of the radicals. The acts, he feared, were ominous precedents that could be followed by more laws designed to keep Americans "in subjection to the Task Master who shall be put over us." The phrase reflected his experience as a slave-owning planter.

By temperament, Henry Laurens was an unlikely revolutionary. Unlike Gadsden, Drayton and Middleton, he did not relish conflict with Britain. He viewed himself as a loyal son of the empire. Laurens had been on bad terms with Gadsden since the first Cherokee War, when both served in the colonial militia. Laurens had defended Colonel James Grant, a Highland

Scots officer Gadsden detested. He clashed with Drayton and Middleton over their encouragement of the violent tactics of the Sons of Liberty. During the Stamp Act Crisis in 1765, a group of Liberty Boys had invaded Laurens's house, searching for stamps. They frightened his ill wife, Eleanor, half to death, he claimed. In desperation, he threw them his cellar keys and told them to help themselves to wine. They found no stamps and left. After Laurens became a Whig leader, he made light of the incident. When the intruders left, he said, they apologized and said, "Bless you, colonel! We hope the poor sick lady will do well." He added that they had done very little damage and were even careful not to step on his flower beds. When the raid happened in 1765, however, he was outraged. He might have remained so, had it not been for an incident two years later. A customs collector recently arrived from Britain, Daniel Moore, ordered the seizure of two of Laurens's ships due to a technical violation of the maritime regulations. Moore enforced the regulations rigidly and benefited from the fines he collected. He made enemies among the Charleston mercantile community. The dispute between Moore and Laurens became acrimonious and personal. Laurens's popularity soared after he publicly twisted Moore's nose. Moore left for England soon after. Laurens sued George Roupell, the customs official who carried out the seizure of his ships. The vice admiralty judge who heard the case, Egerton Leigh, was related to Laurens by marriage. He rendered a compromise judgment that angered both parties. Laurens denounced the verdict as arbitrary because Leigh had not allowed him a jury. Laurens sued Roupell in a local court. A jury awarded him substantial damages Roupell could not pay. During the dispute, Laurens published documents exposing abuses by Leigh. Leigh's reputation, once high, fell. It sank into the mire after he impregnated his ward and sister-in-law, who happened to be Laurens's niece, and then contributed to the death of the child. Laurens denounced Leigh as a wicked fool. The Crown rewarded Leigh for defending British law, making him Sir Egerton Leigh, but many Charlestonians viewed him as a pariah. He went to England in 1774 and never returned.

In the aftermath of the Leigh affair, Laurens became more critical of British colonial policies. Until the summer of 1776, however, he opposed separation from the mother country. In January 1775, he assured a British friend that the Whig goal was only "a reasonable liberty" within the empire. No "sober, sensible man" in America wished for independence. During the debate over the Association in the Second Provincial Congress, he declared himself a loyal subject of the Crown. George III was not to blame for the rift between the colonies and Britain, he said. "Wicked" ministers were. They were the enemies of America and the king. Laurens declared his readiness to battle them to protect liberty and restore the king's right to "reign over a vast empire of freemen." Laurens approved of the Association but opposed efforts to coerce people into subscribing to it. He objected to a clause that labeled those who refused to sign it as persons "inimical to the liberties of America." Many of those persons, he declared, were good citizens who wished well to South Carolina. They shared the concerns of their neighbors but were not ready to support a call to arms. Given time and tolerance, he predicted, many of them would join the struggle for liberty. He refused to consider them enemies: "Our cause is good, it does not stand in need…of sword and fire, to bring men into it…I hate all dogmatic and arbitrary dictates over men's consciences." He compared the clause to rigid Christian doctrines that threatened men with eternal damnation for minor deviations in belief.

At this point, Laurens was treading on dangerous ground. He inserted a parenthetical note in the written speech. "Mr. Parson Tenant very rudely interrupted me." Reverend William Tennent of the Independent Meeting House objected that Laurens was out of order. Laurens denied the objection and tried to proceed. Tennent continued to object, "attempting to confuse me." Laurens responded: "I will speak, I will be heard, or I will be the first man who will refuse to sign your paper.…If I am not heard as a man, I will not sign as your president." In another note, Laurens wrote that Tennent claimed to favor toleration, but "I have found him totally void of charity for other men." Laurens's motion to remove the objectionable clause failed. It remained to provide official sanction to Whig harassment of nonsubscribers. A few days later, Laurens witnessed the tarring and feathering of Dealey and Martin. It disturbed him as all mob actions did, but he did not intervene. He tried to protect friends who refused to subscribe to the Association, but he was no longer captain of the good ship South Carolina. William Henry Drayton was. Laurens had once believed he and other moderates could keep control of events and maintain a firm and steady hold on the tiller. Instead, Drayton and his allies wrested it from them. Laurens faced a dilemma. He was caught between colleagues promoting measures he disapproved of and a diabolical British administration. He viewed Drayton as particularly reckless and unscrupulous. Laurens was horrified by Drayton's scheme to sink old hulks in the harbor to block an invading fleet, fearing it would destroy the seaborne trade Charleston depended on. He ridiculed Drayton's attempts to create a South Carolina navy. Drayton, he fumed, knew nothing about ships or sailing and had purchased guns that were too heavy for the ship he intended to put them on. Laurens's opposition did not matter. Drayton prevailed. In the spring of 1776, Laurens spoke forcefully against Drayton's motion for independence in the Provincial Congress. The majority agreed with Laurens then, but within a few months Drayton had his way on that as well. The Declaration of Independence declared George III a wicked tyrant and vicious enemy of the United States. By accepting it, Laurens became an enemy of the king he had sworn unswerving loyalty to only months before.

Laurens managed to win a victory against Drayton in July 1775. It was a minor victory, except for the individual whose life Laurens may have saved. He was John Burnet, a White Methodist minister. Laurens's reaction to the accusations against Burnet is significant because it contrasted sharply with his reaction to similar accusations against Thomas Jeremiah about the same time. Authorities in St. Bartholomew's Parish had arrested Burnet along with several Blacks on charges of trying to incite a slave insurrection along the Chehaw River. They had received information from a slave named Jemmy that Burnet and several Black preachers had been holding nightly meetings with slaves on local plantations. Jemmy claimed that Burnet preached the equality of all men out of a book that said that God had commanded the king to free them. Jemmy added that he had heard talk of an insurrection in which the slaves would kill all the Whites except Burnet. The St. Bartholomew's justices of the peace ordered the arrested slaves whipped. They hanged one of them, a slave preacher named George, as a warning to other Blacks. They sent Burnet to the Council of Safety in Charleston to be questioned. An accompanying letter of explanation from the parish clerk mentioned that Burnet was a Scot. It ended with "he should have remained in Scotland." Shortly before the council began to interrogate Burnet, another letter arrived from St. Bartholomew's Parish requesting that they remove the words "he should have remained in Scotland" and replace them with "'he should never have come to this province,' to avoid any appearance of national reflections." The vestry had apparently decided that it would be unwise to alienate their Scottish neighbors.

Burnet confessed to preaching to slaves without permission. He denied that he had preached out of any book except the Bible. He spoke only of spiritual equality, he insisted, and never urged the slaves to any action beyond seeking their salvation. Burnet may have been telling the truth. Methodists were a relatively new sect whose leaders, John Wesley and George Whitefield, preached spiritual, not social equality. But history shows that it is but a short step from one to the other. Amid the paranoia gripping the southern colonies in the summer of 1775, many Whites feared their slaves were adopting the dangerous notion that the struggle for liberty applied to them. As Drayton put it, slaves "entertained ideas that the present contest was for obliging us to give them liberty." He and other Whigs blamed the British for putting those ideas in the minds of the enslaved. The truth is that many Blacks had already learned about the Somerset Case through the slave "grapevine" or from hearing Whites complaining about it. The conflict with Britain reinforced the belief that the British were about to free them. To stop the spread of such ideas, Drayton argued, the council should prohibit preaching to slaves. It was best not to give them any ideas at all. God had condemned Blacks to be hewers of wood and drawers of water. To teach them other things was to spoil good field hands. It was especially dangerous to teach them the story of the Hebrews' escape from bondage in Egypt. Laurens replied that everyone, even slaves, should be offered the chance of salvation. Christianity properly taught could reconcile slaves to their worldly position. Drayton wanted to charge Burnet with inciting a slave rebellion, for which he could have been hanged. Laurens replied that he believed Burnet was merely misguided, at most guilty of "a strong tincture of enthusiasm." Moreover, the only evidence against Burnet came from slaves, whose testimony was inadmissible in court. Laurens offered to hire Burnet as an overseer on one of his Georgia plantations, where an eye could be kept on him. Laurens tended to be a bit soft on those he considered men of God. The majority supported Laurens, and the council released Burnet without charge.

Laurens's relaxed view of Burnet's actions contrasts markedly with his reaction to the case of Jeremiah. Whereas Laurens pleaded with his fellow councilors for leniency in Burnet's case, he let justice take its course in Jeremiah's, except in one respect. Other members of the council recommended that the Blacks implicated in the alleged plot be whipped. Laurens argued that they should be released without any punishment if they were found not guilty. But if they were found guilty, the punishment should be death. Laurens subsequently went through contortions to justify Jeremiah's trial and execution. Jeremiah was free. In English law, he was technically entitled to a jury trial. South Carolina law declared slave testimony inadmissible in the trial of a free person, and Jeremiah's accusers, Jemmy and Sambo, were slaves. Laurens denied that these rules applied in Jeremiah's case. English law, he insisted, was designed for Whites. Africans had no claim to its benefits. Thus, a year before the Declaration of Independence, Laurens firmly rejected the document's claim that all men are created equal and entitled to equal rights. Simultaneously, he was arguing that Americans were fighting for liberty and the rights of man. Perhaps he assumed from the beginning that Jeremiah was guilty as charged, and the procedure was less important than the verdict. Laurens made much of the fact that Jeremiah claimed not to know Jemmy, his brother-in-law. While that may seem odd, it was hardly enough to justify hanging someone. Perhaps what Jeremiah meant was, "The man accusing me is not the man I know; the man I know would never have lied about me in this way." Another possibility is that Laurens was unsure of Jeremiah's guilt but deemed his sacrifice expedient. He clearly disliked the man. Jerry, he wrote, was "a forward fellow, puffed up by prosperity, full of vanity and ambition, ruined by luxury and debauchery." That description would have fit some of Laurens's fellow planters. For Laurens, Jeremiah was guilty of being "uppity," trying to rise above his proper station in society. His prominence made him a bad role model for other Blacks. His execution would deter other Blacks from aiding the British. It would also calm anxious, angry Whites. The mob that threatened Governor Campbell helped convince Laurens of the dangers of intervening to stop the execution. Doing so could lead the "low and ignorant," he wrote, to turn on their natural leaders—men like himself. The low and ignorant included his allies, the Sons of Liberty. Ever since they had invaded his house in 1765, he had fretted about the dangers of "mobocracy."

In the febrile atmosphere of 1775, Laurens had reason to be worried. In the autumn, a young man challenged him to a duel. His name was John Grimke. He accused Laurens of having opened letters he had given him to mail. Laurens denied the charge and asked who said he had opened them. Grimke replied, Arthur Middleton and Peter Timothy. Laurens repeated his denial. Grimke accused him of lying and betraying a confidence. He demanded satisfaction on the field of honor. Laurens replied that he did not approve of dueling. Grimke persisted. Laurens gave way. They met on a field on James Island with their seconds. After they walked off the agreed number of paces, they turned around to face each other, pistols in hand. Laurens kept his pistol at his side. Grimke raised his, aimed at Laurens and pulled the trigger. The gun misfired. For an instant, Grimke's courage deserted him. He took several steps back before regaining his composure and returning to his original position. Laurens raised his pistol and pointed it at his challenger. "You are no gentleman!" he shouted. He fired widely on purpose and stormed off the field. In a letter describing the duel, Laurens mentioned that Grimke owed him money. "An honorable man would have repaid the debt before trying to kill his creditor."

Several months before, Laurens had sent his daughters Martha and Mary to England with his brother James. James and his wife had been caring for them since Henry's wife, Eleanor, died in 1770. Presumably, Henry feared for their safety. Why else would he send them away, after just returning from Europe himself? He had not seen them for three years. His sons were already in England for education. He urged them to remain in the country he was accusing of wicked behavior. His eldest son, John, defied him and returned to America, vowing to join the Continental army. John Laurens is remembered today for two things, perhaps three. One is his advocacy of freeing the enslaved to fight against the British during the War for Independence. Another is his tragic and senseless death in one of the last skirmishes of that war. Recently, he has become famous for allegedly having been the more than close friend of Alexander Hamilton. Just how close their friendship was I will leave to others and focus on the first two.

John was Henry's eldest child, born in 1754. When John was seventeen, Henry took him and his two younger brothers to Europe to be educated. Father and son clashed over the latter's program of study. John wished to study medicine. As a boy, he developed a strong interest in medicine and science, which he absorbed from his mentor, Dr. Alexander Garden. Henry insisted that he study law as more suitable to his rank and prospects. John surrendered to his father's wishes and enrolled in one of the ancient English law schools, Lincoln's Inn, in the autumn of 1774. Henry returned to Charleston confident that John was going to pursue the path he had laid out for him. The wheel of history and John's passionate nature combined to produce a different outcome. Henry trusted John to care for his younger brothers. Two events followed that had a scarring effect on John's subsequent life. In the spring of 1776, his brother Jamie died after a fall at his school in Islington. When the fatal accident occurred, John had been with Martha Manning, the daughter of one of Henry's British business associates. John reproached himself for neglecting Jamie. To make matters worse, he impregnated Martha. He married her out of pity, he wrote, rather than for love. Henry was always preaching the importance of self-control, and John believed he had failed his father and brother. Feelings of guilt may have pushed him to return to America immediately, to join in the struggle for independence. He was not the first or last troubled man to seek to redeem himself on the battlefield. Moreover, he had found a mission in the preamble of the Declaration of Independence: "We hold these truths to be self-evident, that all men are created equal, that they are endowed by their Creator with certain unalienable rights, that among these are Life, Liberty, and the Pursuit of Happiness." If those words were to be taken seriously, he believed, Americans would have to abolish slavery. That became a central part of his mission.

Henry urged John to stay in England and take care of his wife and child. He opposed John's plan to enlist in the American army. John was too impulsive and reckless to survive in battle, he claimed. John not only left England but also angered Henry by leaving Martha behind, a few months before she was due to give birth. John arrived in Charleston in the spring of 1777. That summer he traveled to Philadelphia with Henry, who had been elected to the Continental Congress. One would like to have listened in on their conversations on that journey. Henry remained unhappy about John joining the army. But he gave way and used his influence to get his son an "honorable" and, he hoped, safe post. General Washington appointed John as an aide-de-camp. In that position, John formed close friendships with two of Washington's other aides, Alexander Hamilton and the Marquis de Lafayette. John rose quickly to the rank of lieutenant colonel—too quickly in the view of some of his fellow officers. By all accounts he fought bravely in several battles. He was wounded at Germantown and earned a reputation for reckless courage. Lafayette remarked that it was not John's fault he did not get himself killed. In December 1778, John challenged General Charles Lee to a duel after Lee had disparaged Washington. Hamilton served as John's second. John hit Lee in the side with his first shot. He was about to fire again, but the seconds stopped the duel. Lee recovered from his wound and praised John's bravery.

John Laurens, by Charles Wilson Peale, miniature, 1780–81. *U.S. National Portrait Gallery*.

In the spring of 1779, Washington gave John permission to return to South Carolina. He arrived in time to fight against General Prevost's attack from Savannah. When General Moultrie decided to retreat in the face of superior numbers, he sent John with 250 men with orders to bring back a detachment he had left to guard the Coosawatchie River crossing. John ignored Moultrie's instructions and ordered a costly and useless attack. When Prevost reached the outskirts of Charleston and demanded its surrender, Governor Rutledge offered to surrender on the most unusual terms. South Carolina would declare itself neutral if the city was spared occupation. Moultrie and Gadsden vehemently opposed Rutledge's idea, as did John. Prevost rejected them anyway and demanded unconditional surrender. That night he learned Lincoln was marching back to relieve the city and retreated to Savannah, where he prepared strong defensive works, aided by runaways who joined the British in a bid for freedom.

In the autumn, John fought in the combined American and French effort to retake Savannah. Lincoln and his French counterpart, Admiral Count d'Estaing, disagreed and dithered before ordering a last-minute assault on the city's defenses. It was a disaster, the worst American defeat of the war to this point. The French were badly mauled by disease as well as the fighting. Fearing that a hurricane would destroy his fleet, d'Estaing sailed back to France after the battle. According to later accounts, John viewed the attack's failure as a personal dishonor and wished he had been killed. According to a fellow officer, he walked toward the British lines with his arms outstretched as if courting martyrdom. True or not, he was undoubtedly a severely disappointed man at that time, and his dejection may have related to another failure. For John had not come south merely to fight the British. He came to present a startling proposal for the South Carolina State Assembly. He asked its members to raise a regiment of Black soldiers from the enslaved, who would be freed in return for military service. The Continental Congress had approved the plan, provided the South Carolina Assembly concurred. General Lincoln, frustrated by a lack of White enlistments, supported the proposal. Several northern states had enlisted Blacks. With Charleston threatened by a British invasion, the incentive for recruiting Blacks was greater than ever. John pleaded with his father to use his influence on behalf of the scheme. Appealing to Henry's vanity, he stressed the "glory" that would come from "triumphing over deep-rooted national prejudices in favor of country and humanity at large."

The seeds of John's Black regiment project were planted while he was studying law at the Middle Temple in London. He had become acquainted with a pair of young English abolitionists, Thomas Day and John Bicknell. In 1773, they had published "The Dying Negro," a poetic denunciation of slavery, to great acclaim. Day and Bicknell introduced John to Granville Sharp, a passionate crusader against slavery who had brought the case of James Somerset to the courts. All of them supported the American position. Sharp was so incensed by the government's decision to use military force in America that he resigned his government job at the Ordnance Office. But they could not ignore the slavery issue. Day famously wrote, "If there be an object truly ridiculous in nature, it is an American patriot signing a resolution of independence with one hand, and with the other brandishing a whip over his affrighted slave." Influenced by his antislavery friends, John Laurens became a passionate advocate of freedom for all. After reading newspaper reports about the execution of Thomas Jeremiah, he wrote to Henry that if the reports were accurate, "Americans' reputation for justice and humanity must suffer heavily." Imagine Henry's alarm upon reading that. He must have viewed it as an attack on *his* reputation for justice and humanity. He sent John a justification of the execution and asked him to publish it in a London newspaper.

Henry bore the weight of a troubled moral sense. For years he had been trying to exorcise the sins of slave trading from his soul. He never wanted to be a slave merchant, he protested. His father had hated slavery. His brother refused to participate in the slave trade. Henry sought to absolve himself by stressing his personal abhorrence of slavery. In correspondence he described how horrified he was upon learning that a favorite Black playmate had been sold to a planter in Georgetown. He told of discovering the body of a young Black woman who died by suicide after being sold. She was so thin she was able to hang herself with a piece of small vine. "How can anyone who sees such things love the African trade?' he asked. He blamed his mentor, merchant James Crokatt, for his involvement in the slave trade. Crokatt had allegedly promised to make him a partner in his London trading house and then reneged on the promise. Needing to support himself, Henry accepted an opportunity to act as Charleston agent for British West African slave traders. The shift enriched him and saddled him with a nagging conscience.

In August 1776, Henry penned a letter to John explaining his views on the slavery issue. The timing was significant. A copy of the Declaration of Independence had just arrived in Charleston—proof, Henry claimed, that the United States was devoted to liberty and equality. The British, on the other hand, wickedly opposed these things. The tale he told resembles that of a criminal deflecting attention from his crimes by accusing others of worse crimes. He asserted his credentials as a good master. His "negroes" were "strongly attached" to him. None of them had attempted to desert to an enemy whose officers were employing Blacks to pillage plantations. The institution of slavery existed in South Carolina when he was born. The English had established it for their own benefit. Parliamentary laws ensured that they gained most of the profits of slavery and "almost totally prohibited Americans from reaping any share of it." Now the British were stealing the "negroes from the Americans to whom they had sold them." They pretended they were going to "set the poor wretches free." Instead, they were reselling them into far worse slavery in the West Indies. "What meanness! What complicated wickedness appears in this scene! O England how changed! How fallen!" One wonders how John reacted to this parade of righteous indignation. He knew that his father had profited from the slave trade and slave labor on his estates. Was he aware that the claim about British officers selling runaways back into slavery was fabricated? Did he accept Henry's defense or see it as the pot calling the kettle black?

To this point, Henry had countered British accusations of American hypocrisy by charging them with greater hypocrisy. Now he dropped a bombshell. "You know, my dear son, I abhor slavery." He vowed to work to end it, even if it cost him financially: "I am devising means for manumitting many of them, and for cutting off the entail of slavery." He committed himself to this mission. Verbally. Eventually. Vaguely. With a caveat. It would be difficult. "Great powers oppose me." Law, custom and avarice stood in the way. And there was the problem of inheritance. "What will my children say if I deprive them of so much estate?" He might as well have asked, "Think carefully my son, do you want to lose this wealth?" Then he shifted tone again, declaring that these difficulties were "not insuperable." He promised to "do as much as I can in my time and leave the rest to a better hand." It was hypocritical for men to demand liberty for themselves while denying it to others, he conceded. Then one more caveat: "I perceive the work before me is great. I shall appear to many as a promoter not only of strange, but of dangerous doctrines; it will therefore be necessary to proceed with caution." Henry placed himself gingerly in John's camp, while at the same time alerting him that the neighbors would take some convincing.

As if eager to dispose of this disagreeable topic, Henry turned to more pleasant news. He gave an account of the recent Battle of Sullivan's Island. He began by declaring that nothing was more abhorrent to him than "publications of falsehoods for truth." Exactly what he meant by that is hard to say. Perhaps he was warning John not to believe British accounts of events. The inhabitants of Charleston, himself included, had manfully defended the city, except for a few deluded "Tories" and "worse men." No sooner had the battle been won than "the cruel superintendent," Colonel Stuart, had unloosed the Cherokee to commit "ravages and murders" in the backcountry. All these events had strengthened the case for independence. Henry confessed to shedding tears at the idea that the separation from dear old (but wicked) England was permanent. "I am now by the will of God brought into a new world, and God only knows what sort of a world it will be." He ended on an odd note for someone so convinced of British perfidy. He told John to decide for himself which side he would support in the war and remain in England until it ended. Was Henry afraid that his idealistic son's presence in America would make his life more difficult? It did.

Henry's letter to John is in striking contrast to what he had written to a fellow Whig a few months before. In March, Colonel Stephen Bull informed the Council of Safety that hundreds of runaway slaves were taking refuge on Tybee Island in Georgia. Bull requested that the following section not be read out to the Provincial Congress: "It is far better for the public and the owners if the deserted negroes…who are on Tybee Island, be shot, if they cannot be taken." The killing would be best done by Creek Indians, "as it, perhaps, may deter other negroes from deserting, and will establish a hatred or aversion between the negroes and the Indians." On March 16, Laurens sent the council's answer to Bull. It is "an awful business," Laurens wrote, "notwithstanding it has the sanction of law, to put even fugitive and rebellious slaves to death." Nevertheless, the council urged "proper persons to seize and if nothing else will do to destroy all those rebellious negroes upon Tybee Island or wherever they may be found." The "proper persons" might well be Indians, but the council recommended that "discreet white men" lead them. Ordering such "sanguinary measures," Laurens continued, was an "inglorious act," but British "miscreants" made them urgent by "carrying on an inglorious picaroon war." The alternative was to risk the loss of Georgia and perhaps South Carolina and eventually the defeat of "the American cause in which the happiness of ages unborn is included." It was imperative to "perform any act required and warranted by the first law of nature as well as by the law of the land." Here, Henry incorrectly paraphrased Thomas Hobbes or John Locke by stating that the first law of nature was the law of self-preservation. Hobbes's first law of nature holds that men should seek peace with others. Locke's version of the law of nature requires men to seek mutual benefit with others, who all have a natural right to life, liberty and property. The "inglorious acts" Henry approved were obviously not about seeking peace or mutual benefit. Rather, they fell under Hobbes's "Right of Nature, the right of self-preservation." Henry often appealed to the right of self-preservation as a justification for acts that gave him moral qualms.

Henry's letter to John was published in the North in 1861 as proof that some southerners had wanted to abolish slavery in 1776. That may have been true, but the purpose of the letter was to convince John that British accusations of hypocrisy over slavery did not apply to him. In the flush of excitement and idealism over independence, Henry may have believed his own rhetoric. If so, that moment passed quickly. John took his father's words seriously and expected them to lead to action. During the next few years, he pressed Henry on the issue of emancipation. John urged Henry to provide an example to his fellow planters and free his slaves. Blacks shared the same humanity and were entitled to the same natural rights as Whites, John insisted. The degradation of slavery had obscured the parallels in their aspirations and abilities. One can imagine Henry wincing at such words.

In a letter of 1778, Henry promised to give John part of his "inheritance": forty slaves who would receive their freedom and form the nucleus of a unit of free Black soldiers. Henry failed to keep the promise. He was president of the Continental Congress when it debated John's Black regiment proposal in March 1779. The result was a hollow victory. Congress authorized South Carolina and Georgia to raise three thousand Black soldiers *if they believed it practical to do so*. John presented his Black regiment proposal to the South Carolina Assembly three times. The first was in August 1779, only two months after the British had advanced from Savannah to the gates of Charleston before withdrawing. Christopher Gadsden and the Rutledge brothers poured scorn on John's idea. The horrified assembly rejected the proposal by a vote of 60 to 12. Afterward, Henry tried to convince John that his cause was hopeless. He referred to the project as "your black Air Castle" and advised him to find consolation in philosophy. Henry was less concerned about British opinion now, or even John's, and more concerned with that of his neighbors. Unlike John, who had been away for nearly a decade, Henry was acutely sensitive to the mindset of South Carolina's Whites. Most of them were terrified by the idea of freeing and arming Blacks, especially during a war in which so many Blacks had shown a preference for the enemy side. Henry consoled himself by claiming that Whites would be more open to the idea of emancipation after independence and peace had been secured. Whether he believed that or not, it is hard to escape the conclusion that he preferred to pass the problem on to a future generation.

Rejecting his father's advice, John moved his proposal again in early 1780. Clinton was about to begin his siege of Charleston, and the defenders were desperately short of men. General Lincoln supported John's idea, but the assembly declared that it should only be employed "in the last extremity." The last extremity soon arrived, but the proposal was never adopted. After the city's surrender in May, John insisted that the city could have been saved if South Carolina had implemented his Black regiment plan. Opponents of the plan, he declared, loved slavery more than liberty. As if to prove his point, in April 1781 General Thomas Sumter ("The Gamecock") began offering White men a bounty for recruitment: a slave. John remained in Charleston as a prisoner of war until the summer of 1780, when the British paroled him. The parole required him to go to Philadelphia and take no part in the war. He visited briefly with Henry, who was about to leave on a diplomatic mission to the Netherlands. The meeting is unlikely to have been a happy one. In November, John was exchanged for a British officer, which allowed him to resume the fight. He wanted to return to South Carolina immediately. To his dismay, Congress sent him to France with Thomas Paine to seek additional French assistance against Britain. Along with Benjamin Franklin, who had been representing the United States at Versailles since 1777, they convinced Louis XVI to send a fleet and army to America in the summer of 1781. That force played a crucial role in the victory at Yorktown in October. After returning from France, John joined Washington's army at Yorktown, where he fought bravely. Following the battle, John returned to South Carolina and served under General Nathanael Greene. By the time he arrived, the British controlled only Charleston and its environs. At the Jacksonborough Assembly in February 1782, John presented his proposal for establishing a Black regiment for the third and final time. Delegates heaped ridicule on it. One opponent presented an argument echoed throughout the South during the next century and more. He denounced it as a half-baked northern plan to encourage race mixing. Think of the dangers it poses to your daughters and the blood of your grandchildren, he warned. Others elaborated on the horrors of armed, masterless "Negroes" roaming the countryside. The assembly rejected the proposal by a large margin. John was devastated. He realized that this was probably his last chance to win support for his plan. The war was all but over. A couple of years earlier, he had written that if South Carolina could not be cultivated without slaves, "we should flee from it as a hateful country." We will never know how seriously he meant those words. He was killed in one of the last actions of the war, a senseless skirmish along the Combahee River in August 1782. John was commanding a detachment of soldiers when they encountered a much larger British force foraging for food. Impulsive as always, he ignored an order to wait for reinforcements and launched an immediate attack. He died leading the charge, aged twenty-seven.

Henry did not learn of John's death for three months. In September 1780, a British frigate captured him at sea on his way to the Netherlands with the draft of a treaty of alliance with the Dutch. His captors took him to England. The government lodged him in the Tower of London on suspicion of treason. Henry Laurens has the distinction of being the only American to have been imprisoned in that ancient fortress. As he entered the Tower through Traitor's Gate, the guards serenaded him with a rendition of "Yankee Doodle Dandy." He remained more than a year, his treatment alternating between harsh and mild. After Yorktown, it improved considerably. The British government hoped to exchange him for Lord Cornwallis, now an American prisoner. Laurens was permitted the services of his body slave, George. Two British artists, John Singleton Copley and Lemuel Abbott, painted his portrait. He was allowed visitors. William Manning, an old friend and John's father-in-law, came along with John's wife, Martha, and the couple's four-year-old daughter, Frances. Another visitor was Richard Oswald, Laurens's former partner in the slave trade. Laurens had been Charleston agent for the slave "factory" at Bunce Island, Sierra Leone, in which Oswald was heavily invested. Oswald had close connections to high-ranking politicians. In December 1781, he put up bail in the enormous sum of £100,000 to secure Henry's release from the Tower. Ironically, the judge who granted his release was Lord Mansfield of the Somerset Case. Soon afterward, the British exchanged Henry Laurens for Cornwallis. Now that he was free to leave, Congress appointed him to the American peace delegation at Paris. The other delegates, John Adams, John Jay and Benjamin Franklin, were all from northern states. The trio began negotiations in April 1782. Laurens remained in England for another seven months, pleading ill health. He went to Bath, England's most fashionable health spa, to "take the waters." In November, he received a letter from Adams informing him of John's death. Adams urged him to come to Paris immediately. He arrived on November 30, one day before the preliminary treaty was to be signed. Despite his absence from the negotiations, Henry insisted on adding a clause to the treaty. It stipulated that the British government return all runaway slaves to their American masters. British generals had promised the runaways freedom, but it happened that the chief British negotiator in Paris was Laurens's old slave trading partner, Richard Oswald. He accepted Laurens's

*Left*: Henry Laurens, by John Singleton Copley, circa 1781. *U.S. National Portrait Gallery.*

*Right*: Henry Laurens, by Lemuel Abbott, 1781. *Courtesy U.S. Senate Art Collection.*

addition, and it went into the final draft of the treaty. It is hard not to suspect that Laurens and Oswald had cut a deal. In subsequent correspondence, Oswald asked Laurens to find him some good plantation land in Georgia or South Carolina. By insisting on the insertion of the runaway clause, Henry betrayed his promise to John that he would work to end slavery. Perhaps he felt that John's death released him from his pledge. Perhaps he bever intended to honor it.

After signing the preliminary peace treaty, Henry returned to England, the country he had so often denounced as wicked. He served briefly as temporary U.S. ambassador to Great Britain. In 1784, he returned to South Carolina after nearly six years' absence. He never returned to politics. The state assembly selected him as a delegate to the U.S. Constitutional Convention in 1787, but he declined. During his remaining years, he devoted himself to restoring his estates, especially his beloved Mepkin Plantation, which the British had burned during their occupation. In 1785, he brought his orphaned granddaughter Frances (Fanny) to South Carolina. John's sister Martha and her husband, David Ramsay, raised her in their family. She married twice and died in South Carolina, aged eighty-three. Henry died at Mepkin in 1792, surrounded by his "faithful" servants. He suffered from taphophobia, the fear of being buried alive. In his will, he stipulated that his body be cremated. It was possibly the first cremation of a European in the United States. John Laurens is also buried at Mepkin, now the home of a Trappist monastery. John's gravestone is important for what it says and doesn't say. For the epitaph, Henry chose a martial line from the Roman poet Horace, one taught to many British schoolboys: "Dulce et decorum est, pro patria mori." ("It is sweet and proper to die for one's country.") It seems an odd choice, given that Henry had tried to keep John out of the army. The grave says nothing about John's antislavery sentiments. Apparently, Henry buried those along with his son. Henry freed one of his slaves in his will. Perhaps that was enough to ease his conscience.

How sincere was John in advocating emancipation? Was he making a grand but futile gesture? Was he trying salve his conscience over slavery and his failings as a brother, husband and father? Did he court death in despair at the failure of his country and father to live up to the ideals of the Declaration of Independence? It is impossible to be sure of these things. What can be said is that no southerner during the revolution made a more forceful argument for emancipation than John Laurens. When his opponents claimed that Blacks were incapable of appreciating and handling liberty, he countered that Blacks and Whites shared the same humanity, abilities and desires. Slavery had debased a people who, under better circumstances, would prove to be excellent citizens of the republic: "We have sunk the Africans and their descendants below the Standard of Humanity, and almost rendered them incapable of that Blessing [Liberty] which equal Heaven bestowed upon us all." During the early nineteenth century, southern writers extolled John Laurens as a brave and chivalric model for the region's youth, but like John's grave marker, they suppressed his emancipationist views. In the 1860s, hundreds of thousands of southern men died for a cause far less worthy than his.

# ALEXANDER GARDEN

People who supported the British government during the American Revolution were a diverse lot. Loyalists were rich, poor, men, women, White, Black, Native American and mixed race. Many Loyalists had family who supported the opposing side. William Franklin, the royal governor of New Jersey, was the illegitimate son of Benjamin Franklin. The lieutenant governor of British East Florida, Dr. John Moultrie Jr., was the brother of Patriot hero William Moultrie. Some Loyalists kept a low profile and tried to get on with life. Others, like George Milligen, were belligerent in their loyalty. One who outdid even Milligen was Charles Webb of St. Paul's Parish, a few miles southwest of Charleston. On July 18, 1775, the St. Paul's Committee of Safety reported Webb to a justice of the peace for "malicious expressions said against the lieutenant governor (William Bull) and the committees." One witness said Webb had called Bull "a damned fool" for not declaring war on the rebels. Several witnesses claimed to have heard Webb declare "he would go to England and take a commission and come against the Americans." Webb boasted that he "could take the whole province if he had a regiment of the king's soldiers, for he well knew that the Americans would not fight." Webb denounced the St. Paul's committee as "a set of mechanical, ignorant rascals" consisting of "butchers, tailors & cobblers." He wished the British navy would "take them prisoners and carry them to England to be treated as rebels," for they were greater "rebels than ever the Scotch were." Here, Webb was referring to the Jacobite rebellions. He made an insightful remark about the effects of the rebellions on the political calculations of many Scots in 1775. He was not surprised that the Scots were "such loyal subjects, for a burnt child would dread the fire." Experience taught them the folly of rebelling against the Hanoverian monarchy. The "rascals of property" in South Carolina who ignored that lesson would look foolish when their lands and "Negroes" were forfeit to the king. It was a pity that there "wasn't a gallows in Charlestown to hang all the Americans." As for the St. Paul's committee, they "were a lousy set of blackguards." The committee declared Webb an enemy to South Carolina.

Alexander Garden took a far more guarded stance than Webb or Milligan toward the rebellion. He refused to support it but did not openly oppose it. Until 1780 at least, he claimed to be neutral. In this he was not unusual. Many colonists found it difficult to choose a side during the revolution. They tried to avoid supporting or offending the warring parties. The poet Dante may have reserved a spot in hell for neutrals, but Americans often chose neutrality for reasons of conscience, not cowardice. The Quakers refused to fight for either side for religious reasons. Garden's reasons were political.

Most writing about Garden centers on his contributions to natural history. Historians of science consider him one of the most important colonial scientists. My focus here is on his attempts to negotiate the treacherous waters of revolutionary America, a subject that has received much less attention. Garden was born in Birse, Aberdeenshire, Scotland, in 1730, the son of the minister of the village church. He studied medicine at Aberdeen and Edinburgh Universities and enlisted in the British navy as a surgeon. After several years, he resigned due to seasickness and a lung complaint, perhaps tuberculosis. The air below decks was always foul, and Garden believed the miasma was killing him. He made only two long trips by sea after leaving the navy. The first was when he immigrated to South Carolina in 1752. Rich and sickly, Charleston was a magnet for doctors. Scotland, which produced far more medical men than it could employ, supplied most of the demand. The bulk of Charleston's medical corps in the decades before the revolution was born in Scotland, of Scottish lineage or trained in Scotland. As one of the town's Scottish physicians put it, "Physic is a fine traveling business." A medical man could earn a good income in Charleston if he didn't succumb to the diseases that killed so many of his patients. Garden suffered from the local fevers as nearly all newcomers did. But he survived what Carolinians called "The Seasoning," the initial bouts of malaria and possibly yellow fever and dysentery as well. A few years after arriving, he wooed and wed a young heiress of Huguenot lineage, Elizabeth Peronneau. He called her Toby. Three of their children survived to adulthood: a son, Alex, and two daughters, Harriette and Juliette.

By the early 1760s, Garden had developed a flourishing practice. His reputation and income grew in part from his skill at inoculating for smallpox, the most dreaded scourge of colonial America. In January 1760, a major smallpox epidemic struck Charleston. The demand for inoculation, which had proved its value during a previous epidemic in 1738, was huge. Garden wrote that "many more people were inoculated than could be attended by the practitioners of physic." He estimated that 2,400 to 2,800 people were inoculated in less than two weeks, about one-fourth of the population. Inoculation was profitable. During a less virulent epidemic in 1763, Garden inoculated more than 1,000 people. On the eve of the revolution, he was one of the richest physicians in town. He acquired several properties in Charleston and beyond and established a network of friends and clients among the colonial elite. He became a close friend of Henry Laurens and mentored Henry's son John. In his spare time, Garden pursued his passion for natural history. He corresponded with and sent botanical and zoological specimens to natural historians in Europe, including the Swede Linnaeus, who developed the modern system of biological classification. In 1760, Linnaeus named a highly scented flowering plant after Garden, the *gardenia.* Ironically, it was not anything Garden had discovered or described. It came from South Africa.

Honors and recognition piled up. In 1768, the American Philosophical Society and the American Society for Promoting and Propagating Useful Knowledge elected him a corresponding member. A greater accolade came in 1773. The Royal Society of London, one of the most prestigious scientific societies in the Western world, elected Garden to membership. Among the members who nominated him was Benjamin Franklin, then working in London as a colonial agent. When John Moultrie Jr. became lieutenant governor of British East Florida in 1773, Garden bought his Goose Creek plantation. Garden renamed it Otranto, probably after Horace Walpole's recently published gothic novella, *The Castle of Otranto*. At Otranto, Garden experimented with landscaping using local plants and pioneered in American landscape design.

Within two years, the hurricane of revolution arrived and began to demolish Garden's comfortable world. It did not catch him by surprise. He understood the seriousness of the issues dividing the colonies and Britain during the Stamp Act Crisis ten years before. Those who rejected

Otranto Plantation historical marker, Goose Creek, South Carolina. *Author's collection.*

Parliament's right to legislate for the colonies, he wrote, were demanding sovereignty. In the summer of 1775, the Whigs pressed him to sign the Association. For Garden, as for many in the colonies, it was a genuine dilemma. He sympathized with colonial grievances, but he did not share the Whigs' optimism that separation from Britain would improve their lives. Charlestonians were already among the most prosperous inhabitants of the empire. A struggle for independence would imperil that prosperity. Personally, he feared that war and its disorders would disrupt the calm philosophic study of the creation. For Garden, natural history was a form of religious contemplation. There was yet another reason. When he joined the Royal Navy, he had taken an oath of allegiance to the British Crown. He believed that signing the Association would violate his oath and could open him to charges of treason. During his youth in Scotland, he had witnessed the costs of joining a rebellion against the Crown, the Jacobite Revolt of 1745. His father, the minister of Birse, had remained loyal to the Hanoverian king, George II. People who supported Prince Charles Edward Stuart (Bonnie Prince Charlie) lost their land, their freedom and often their lives.

Garden received some protection from friends among the Whig elite, particularly Henry Laurens. When Laurens opposed harsh measures against persons who refused to sign the Association, he was probably thinking of Garden, among others. Laurens tried to convince Garden to sign but failed. The Liberty Boys used sterner tactics. Garden was ill from a fever when a group of them barged into his bedroom and demanded he sign the Association. He signed with a caveat. He would revoke his support if he learned it violated his oath of allegiance to the Crown. He refused Whig offers to take a post in the army medical service.

Garden's situation became more precarious after independence. The assembly passed a law requiring people to swear allegiance to the state or leave. Laurens warned Garden that neutrality was now being viewed the same as opposition to American independence. He advised Garden to get a certificate from a friendly magistrate that would satisfy the authorities. Garden found a magistrate who certified that he swore to promote the "real and true interests of Carolina to the utmost of his ability." Vague as it was, Whig leaders accepted it. Their willingness to do so owed much to Garden's reputation as a skilled physician with an elite clientele. Eliza Pinckney and Dorothy Drayton, among others, sought his medical advice and prescriptions. Getting paid for his work became increasingly difficult. Rampant inflation, food shortages, embargoes on exports and a lack of investment capital brought privation for many and true suffering for others. Many families were unable or unwilling to pay their medical bills or paid Garden in nearly worthless state paper currency. In 1775, he had loaned more than £2,000 in South Carolina currency to the Shubrick family. The amount was then equivalent to £320 sterling. In 1779, Thomas Shubrick repaid the loan in currency now worth £7 sterling. As a hedge against inflation, Garden invested in indigo, which became a kind of wartime currency. Unfortunately, the casks of indigo he shipped off were seized by British privateers. The great fire of January 1778 severely damaged his house on Broad Street. While it was being repaired, he moved his family temporarily to another house he owned.

For five turbulent years, Garden negotiated the treacherous political waters of revolutionary Charleston. On several occasions, he considered leaving for Britain but never went, partly because he dreaded another long voyage. The British seizure of Charleston in May 1780 changed his situation, potentially at least. He could have openly declared himself a Loyalist. Sir Henry Clinton issued a proclamation offering a pardon for "treasonable offenses" to persons who signed an Oath of Loyalty to the British Crown. The crowd that flocked to Clinton's headquarters at the Miles Brewton House to take the oath included Rawlin Lowndes, Charles Pinckney, Henry Middleton and Gabriel Manigault. Garden was not among them. Perhaps he reasoned that he had never committed a treasonable offense, and he had taken an oath of allegiance when he joined the British navy. He refused offers to take a position on the Board of Police, which the British set up to administer civilian affairs in Charleston.

Garden officially abandoned his neutrality a few months after the fall of Charleston. In August, Lord Cornwallis routed a larger American army at Camden. Many people believed his victory solidified British control of South Carolina and Georgia. In the aftermath of the battle, Charleston Loyalists drafted a memorial of congratulations to the victor. Garden signed it. Perhaps he genuinely believed that it was now safe to express Loyalist views. Or perhaps he was pressured to do so. Cabinet-maker Thomas Elfe claimed he signed because John Wells, who had changed sides twice since 1776, had threatened him. Whether Garden signed under duress or willingly, congratulations were premature. Camden proved to be the high-water mark of British success in the Southern Campaign. Disease, partisan attacks and the arrival of another Continental army under General Nathanael Greene undermined the British position in the Carolinas during the next few months. Of these, disease was more important than most historical accounts have allowed. The British army's strength was depleted by malarial fevers, dysentery and possibly yellow fever. Native or long resident Carolinians had an advantage over the British when it came to the local fevers—something epidemiologists call differential immunity. People who had been born in or lived in the state for years had often developed a degree of immunity or resistance to malarial and other fevers. They might get ill, but they were less likely to be severely debilitated or die than the "unseasoned" British soldiers, and they would generally recover the ability to function more quickly. The number of British effectives was reduced considerably by fevers in the summer and autumn of 1780. Even at Camden, about one-third of the army was unable to fight due to sickness. Cornwallis was critically ill with a fever when the Overmountain Men annihilated a Loyalist detachment at King's Mountain in October. During this period, partisans led by Francis Marion and Thomas Sumter began disrupting British supply lines and attacking isolated detachments. General Daniel Morgan routed a British detachment under Banastre Tarleton at Cowpens in January 1781.

Disease and partisan attacks continued to deplete British strength during the following months. Cornwallis moved into North Carolina after the New Year hoping to enlist Loyalists there, but few joined his army. In March, he defeated Greene at Guilford Courthouse, but he took heavy losses and retreated toward Wilmington. In April, Cornwallis decided to march his battered army north to Virginia. Among the reasons he gave for the move was that he could not subject his men to another deadly summer in feverish South Carolina. His decision led to Yorktown and defeat that October. The British and Loyalist forces Cornwallis left behind in South Carolina under Lord Rawdon were insufficient to control the backcountry. When Cornwallis moved north, Greene went around him into South Carolina. Rawdon repulsed Greene's Continentals at Hobkirk's Hill in April, but like Guilford Courthouse, it was a Pyrrhic victory. During the next few months, partisan harassment and Greene's cautious advances forced British and Loyalist forces to retreat toward the coast and Charleston. Ill and exhausted, Rawdon arrived in Charleston in late July and left for Britain soon after. A few weeks after his departure, Greene's army fought a British force to a standstill at Eutaw Springs. Both sides claimed victory, but the British retreated to the perimeter of Charleston. Eutaw Springs was the last major battle of the war in South Carolina, although skirmishing continued for another year.

When the British evacuated Charleston in December 1782, Garden left with them. He dreaded the journey but had no choice. The Jacksonborough Assembly banished him and confiscated most of his property because he had signed the memorial congratulating Cornwallis after the Battle of Camden. John Laurens tried but failed to get Garden's punishment reduced to a fine. After the British evacuation, the new governor of South Carolina, John Matthews, occupied Garden's house on Broad Street.

The War for Independence proved disastrous for Garden in another, not uncommon way. It divided his family. His daughter Harriette fell in love with a British officer, Major George Benson. They married in St. Michael's Church in February 1781. Garden had reason to be uneasy about the marriage. Benson was the officer who had carried out the arrests of the rebels Nisbet Balfour sent to St. Augustine in the summer of 1780. A few months after Harriette's marriage, Garden's son, Alex, returned from a decade of education in Britain. Garden urged him to remain there until the war ended, but Alex insisted on returning. After he arrived, Garden gifted him Otranto, his plantation at Goose Creek. After Alex moved there, he mysteriously disappeared. Garden received a letter from him a few weeks later. It came from the camp of General Nathanael Greene. Alex

Alexander Garden's House, Broad Street, Charleston. *Author's collection.*

claimed that a detachment of Continental cavalry had arrived at Otranto, asking for Dr. Garden. Greene's army, their commander explained, was suffering heavy losses from fevers and needed medical assistance. Alex replied that his father was in Charleston. The officer told him to come with them. Was Alex kidnaped or did he go willingly? In any case, he left and, after meeting with Greene, accepted an offer to enlist as an ensign. He rose to the rank of major by the end of the war. Because he had joined the army, the state assembly allowed him to keep Otranto. Some delegates suspected that he had enlisted to save the family property. The possibility cannot be ignored. During the Jacobite rebellions in Scotland, some families had used such a strategy to keep their estates whatever the outcome of the struggle. Dr. Garden denied any collusion with Alex to both the American and British governments. He denounced Alex's decision to join Greene's army and never fully reconciled with him. South Carolina later restored some of Dr. Garden's property and rescinded his banishment, but he never returned to Charleston. Alex married Mary Anna Gibbes, daughter of one of his father's old friends, and wrote two books about the American Revolution. When he died in 1829, Otranto passed to his adopted nephew Alester Gibbes. Dr. Garden settled in the West End of London, in a house just off the Strand. He became an active and popular member of the Royal Society and was elected vice-president. Like many others exiled by the revolution, he applied to the Loyalist Claims Commission seeking compensation for his losses. The amount the Commission awarded him was well below his claim, and it did not come until shortly before his death in 1791 of a lung disorder. In 1784, Garden wrote to fellow naturalist Thomas Pennant explaining the effects of the war on his life. A political tempest had "torn him up by the roots." But what he regretted most was the loss of years he could have devoted to natural history. The war, he wrote, had almost destroyed his love of learning. Garden's loss was also a loss to American science.

# SCIPIO HANDLEY

In 1775, Scipio Handley was a Black fisherman plying his trade in Charleston Harbor. We know little else about him, except that he became involved in the revolutionary struggle on the British side. After the war, he applied for compensation to the Loyalist Claims Commission in London. The memorial Handley submitted to the commission provides most of what we know about him. It is one of thousands of documents about Loyalists that survive in the UK National Archives at Kew. Handley's memorial claimed he was free and had owned property in Charleston. His first service to Britain occurred after Lord William Campbell fled Charleston in September 1775. It was only a few weeks after his fellow fisherman Thomas Jeremiah was hanged. Perhaps motivated by Jeremiah's fate, Handley used his fishing boat to carry supplies and messages to Campbell's ships. He took Lady William Campbell to join her husband when she fled Charleston a few weeks later.

In performing these acts, Handley risked his life. After Lord William fled, the Council of Safety prohibited any boats going to the British ships without a pass from them. Handley avoided Whig patrols by going at night when the moon was down or when it was cloudy. But one night a patrol intercepted him. The council charged him with being a spy. According to Henry Laurens, Arthur Middleton wanted to hang Handley immediately. Most of the council agreed. Laurens replied that he should be hanged if guilty, but only after a proper trial. Exactly what would have constituted a proper trial in the wake of the Jeremiah affair is worth pondering. We

Black soldier fighting with the British, 1781. *The Death of Major Peirson* by John Singleton Copley. *Courtesy Tate Images.*

will never know. Handley escaped from captivity one night shortly before Christmas and disappeared. In his memorial, he claimed that in escaping he had jumped from a second-story window and landed badly, suffering a rupture. In severe pain, he made his way to the runaway camp on Sullivan's Island. When the Whigs broke that up, he went to St. Augustine with Lord William Campbell. From there, he made his way to Barbados and resumed life as a fisherman. He remained in Barbados three years.

After the British captured Savannah in December 1778, they recruited Handley to serve as a Black Pioneer. They put him to work making munitions, a smelly and dangerous job. General Prevost armed him, along with other Black men, to help defend against Savannah against the American and French assault on the city in the autumn of 1779. Handley claimed that the "Negroes" did everything they could to repel the attackers. They knew that the rebels would show no mercy to them if the British surrendered. Handley was shot in the leg while carrying grapeshot to the artillery. It took months for the wound to heal enough so that he could walk. He would have taken part in the British siege of Charleston the following spring, he declared, if he had been able. At the time he submitted his memorial to the Loyalist Claims Commission, he stated that he remained unable to walk properly. The pain was so bad at times he could not work. He requested £97 from the Claims Commission as compensation for the loss of his boat, seven hogs and furniture. The value of his claim would be about $25,000 in today's money. That may seem substantial, but many White Loyalists claimed thousands of pounds. When the commissioners interviewed Handley, he brought along a White woman to testify on his behalf. Eleanor Lister was a Charleston widow. She had made and sold pies and sometimes traded pies for fish from Handley. Lister testified that she believed he was free and that he had possessed at least some of what he claimed. When one of the commissioners asked what kind of furniture Handley possessed, she answered: "Good enough for Negroes." She asked the commission to compensate him because he had "risked his life to serve His Majesty." The commission eventually awarded him £20. That was the maximum awarded to Black Loyalists, and only to those who could prove they had owned some property. Those who had none received nothing but their freedom. The minimum award for White Loyalists was £25. Many received much more.

# THE WANDERING WELLS FAMILY

One of the most compelling narratives produced by a Loyalist during the War for Independence was written by a woman, Louisa Susannah Wells. She left a detailed record of her voyage into exile from Charleston in 1778. *The Journal of a Voyage from Charlestown, S.C., to London* provides a rare glimpse into the experiences of Charleston Loyalists during the Revolutionary War era. Louisa was born in Charleston in 1755. Her parents, Robert Wells and Mary Rowand Wells, had recently emigrated from Scotland. Five of their children survived to adulthood: John, Priscilla, Louisa, William Charles and Helena.

Robert had trained as a bookbinder in Scotland. In Charleston, he diversified. He opened a bookstore and stationery shop, the Great Stationery and Book Store, at the corner of Elliott Street and Bedon's Alley and began to import large numbers of books. His innovations revolutionized the book trade in the Carolinas. He not only increased the variety of books available but also found ways to reduce their price. By the mid-1750s, he was advertising that he could import any work printed in Britain. He later claimed to have as large a stock of books as any bookseller in the colonies. In 1758, he acquired a printing press and began to produce books, almanacs and pamphlets. In the same year, he and another Scots printer, David Bruce, established Charleston's second newspaper, the *South Carolina Weekly Gazette*. In 1764, Wells became sole proprietor and renamed it the *South Carolina and American General Gazette.*

Wells was a Latin scholar well read in history and literature. He printed poems, articles and satires from the London press in his paper. In addition, he

Louisa Susannah Wells Aikman. Painting by Nalan Laluk, copied from portrait in Wells's *Journal of a Voyage from Charleston to London*, 1778, New York, 1906.

developed a lucrative business as a vendue master or commissioned auctioneer. He was active in community affairs. He became the General Secretary of the local order of Masons, joined the Charleston Library Society and the St. Andrews Society. Through his connections to government officials, he acquired various posts in the vice admiralty courts. He invested in Charleston real estate and purchased three thousand acres of land in the province. One of the houses he owned survives at the southwest corner of Tradd and East Bay Streets. By 1775, he had amassed a tidy fortune and made powerful enemies. The coming of the revolution disrupted his business empire. Wells made things difficult for himself by attacking the "disloyal principles" of the Whigs in his *Gazette*. He lampooned Whig hero John Wilkes. When Charleston's Whigs cheered news of the Boston Tea Party, Robert condemned it as a mob action. In the same issue (May 13, 1774), he warned of the dangers of mob rule in reporting an event in the backcountry town of Ninety-Six. A crowd had stormed the jail and freed a prisoner accused of murdering an Indian. Many years later, his son William recalled that he made himself "extremely offensive" through "constantly maintaining the cause of royalty."

Wells was sincere in his loyalism, but he benefited from his connections to the royal administration. There was also a personal side to the positions he took. As the printer of a newspaper, he competed with Peter Timothy, who printed Charleston's oldest newspaper, the *South Carolina Gazette*. Timothy was a close friend of Scottophobe Christopher Gadsden. Timothy published Wilkes's anti-Scottish essays and accused Wells of benefiting from his Scottish connections. The coming of the revolution sharpened their rivalry. Timothy praised Whig actions and principles in his newspaper. He was an active member of the Sons of Liberty, whose harassment led Wells to leave for London. William Wells wrote that his father found it "prudent" to leave in the summer of 1775. William joined him in London a few months later. His mother, Mary, and sisters Priscilla and Helena soon followed. John and Louisa remained in Charleston to run the family businesses.

In one of the many ironies of the revolution, Robert Wells's newspaper was the first in South Carolina to publish the Declaration of Independence. Before 1775, John Wells had apparently shared his father's Loyalist views. But he signed the Association and pressed William to sign. John's conversion may have been motivated by business calculation, Whig harassment or both. A liberty mob closed Wells's shop briefly in the summer of 1775, but events soon opened a new opportunity. One of his journalistic competitors, Charles Crouch, died in 1775. His newspaper died with him. Peter Timothy became so involved in Whig politics that he closed his newspaper the same year. From three newspapers, Charleston was down to one, and Wells's *Gazette* was the one. Sensing opportunity, John removed his father's name from the masthead in 1776. In a letter to Henry Laurens, he declared allegiance to the revolution and virtually disowned his family. He expressed regret and embarrassment at being "connected by friendship and even blood to several who are now our public enemies." At Laurens's request, John published the Declaration of Independence after a copy arrived in Charleston in early August 1776. He published other Whig polemics, joined the Continental army and fought at Savannah. When the British captured Charleston in 1780, however, John rediscovered his love for the Crown. He enlisted in the Loyalist militia and claimed he had joined the Whigs under duress. His newspaper became a mouthpiece of loyalism, and he pressured others to declare allegiance to the Crown. In 1782, with British control over South Carolina nearing its end, he went to England. From there, he relocated, first to Florida, then to the Bahamas, where he published a newspaper. In 1791, he appealed his banishment from South Carolina. If he returned, it was unlikely to have been for long. He died in the Bahamas in 1799.

John's flexible approach to loyalty kept the Wells business intact but alienated him from his family. Louisa was an unwavering Loyalist who essentially disowned him. She never mentions him in the journal. The journal's appendix contains more than fifty documents relating to the Wells family. None of them mention John by name. In 1778, Louisa and John parted ways forever. She joined a group of Loyalists leaving for Britain, many of them officially banished. A catastrophic fire in Charleston that January had destroyed much of the Wells family property. The state government confiscated much of the rest. Louisa had promised her father that she would stay in Charleston to safeguard his property "as long as one stone stood upon another." She no longer felt bound by that promise. Her father's attorneys recommended she leave for Britain. As we shall see, she had another reason for wanting to go. In late June, Louisa, her uncle Robert Rowand, his son and other Loyalists boarded the ship *Providence*, bound for Rotterdam. From there, they planned to get passage to England. Louisa brought her maid Bella with her. Presumably, Bella was enslaved, which raises the question, did Bella want to leave? Did she know, as many slaves knew, that the Somerset decision could make her legally free once she landed in Britain?

As the ship was leaving Charleston Harbor, boats were bringing palmetto trees into town to celebrate the second anniversary of what Louisa called the "ever inglorious 28th of June 1776." She meant the Battle of Sullivan's Island. As the ship passed Fort Sullivan, now renamed Fort Moultrie, at the entrance to the harbor, the passengers could see British cannon balls "lodged in the [palmetto] logs as in a sponge." The ship remained stuck at the harbor entrance for several days by adverse winds. On July 1, it went bumpily but safely over the treacherous sand bar at the entrance to the harbor. A Black harbor pilot named Bluff guided the ship through the obstacle. The grateful passengers paid him $100 in addition to the ship master's fee. Louisa remarked on Bluff's skill and added that the passengers had purposely selected a Black pilot in preference to a White man. The year before another group of Loyalists trying to leave had used a White pilot who ran their ship aground on the bar. The accident, if that's what it was, delayed their departure for months. The passengers on the *Providence* suspected that rebels had bribed the White pilot to strand the ship on the sands. Bluff told them he supported the British. Once on the open ocean, the passengers celebrated their deliverance from "the dominion of Congress." As they sailed away on a brisk southwest wind, the last bit of Charleston to disappear was the steeple of St. Michael's. More hair-raising adventures lay ahead. On the Fourth of July (how ironic!), a British frigate, *The Rose*, overtook and captured their vessel. The captain of *The Rose*, James Reid, at first thought *Providence* was French. In fact, it had been built in France. Once he boarded it, he concluded that the passengers were American rebels. Despite the passengers' protests of loyalty, he ordered *Providence* taken as a prize, hoping to claim its cargo as the spoils of war. He escorted the ship to the British stronghold of New York City. On the way, a French squadron pursued them, but Reid managed to outrun it.

The British authorities in New York initially treated the passengers as rebels. At one point, the men on board *Providence* were about to be sent to a prison ship. They were saved by local friends who identified them as

Loyalists. They could not leave, however, until a vice admiralty court ruled on whether *Providence* was a legitimate prize. If it did, the passengers would forfeit their possessions. After several weeks, the court ruled that *Providence* was not a legitimate prize. The passengers recovered their property and were allowed to leave for Britain. In mid-October, they embarked on the *Mary and Charlotte*, accompanied by a convoy of naval and mercantile ships. After having survived several storms and avoided French and American privateers, the ships became lost in dense fog for eight days off the south English coast. When the fog cleared, they found themselves off the rocky, treacherous coast of Cornwall. That night, another ferocious storm struck. Five of the six ships in their group sank in the storm. Louisa's ship survived and anchored off Dover on November 27. Contrary winds prevented their landing there, but they were able to disembark not far down the coast at Deal. Observing the thick stone walls of Deal Castle, Louisa remarked that the British should build forts of palmetto logs.

She described her emotions when finally stepping onto "British soil": "I could have kissed the gravel on the salt beach! It was my home: the country which I had so long and so earnestly wished to see. The Isle of Liberty and Peace." It was an ironic statement from a woman born in South Carolina of Scottish parents arriving on the south coast of England for the first time. Her phrase "The Isle of Liberty and Peace" shows that neither side in the war had a monopoly on exaggerated patriotic rhetoric. Louisa proceeded overland to London and the home of her parents on Fleet Street, where Robert had established a printing business. Louisa fell ill of a fever after she arrived. Her physicians ordered her to go to Bath Spa to "take the waters." As fans of Jane Austen will know, many families took marriageable daughters to Bath to find a suitable husband. Louisa's journey was probably just health related. She remarked that she would have preferred to voyage to the West Indies, a clue to her next move. She ended her journal at this point, but from the appendix, we learn that she made another long voyage in 1781, this time to Jamaica. She went to marry Alexander Aikman, a Scottish printer who had worked for her father in Charleston. A firm Loyalist, Aikman left for Jamaica in 1777, where he established a newspaper and prospered as a printer. Louisa's voyage to Jamaica proved almost as adventurous as the one to London. A French ship captured hers. The French interned her for several months before releasing her to complete her journey. She married Aikman in January 1782. He became a substantial planter owning hundreds of slaves. The couple had ten children. Only four survived to adulthood. Around 1801, Louisa moved back to England, to the Isle of Wight, to care for one of her daughters. She died there in 1831, aged seventy-six. She left behind a songbook she had created. It contained more than one hundred song sheets her father had brought to Charleston. The songbook is now housed in the Music Division of the Library of Congress.

Many of the documents in the journal's appendix relate to William Charles Wells, Louisa's younger brother, whom she admired. After he died, she erected a memorial to William and her parents at St. Bride's Church on Fleet Street. German bombs destroyed the memorial during World War II, but the inscription is recorded in the appendix. It states that William expanded the bounds of natural science. Indeed, William Charles Wells is one of those figures in medical and scientific history who should be better known than he is. Like so many others, revolution disrupted his life. When he was a boy, his father sent him out dressed in a tartan jacket and a blue Scots bonnet. In a memoir, William explained that Robert was trying to make him into a true Scotsman and inoculate him against "disloyal principles." Given the anti-Scottish feelings among some Charlestonians, this fashion statement made William's boyhood difficult. Children teased and persecuted him. To escape, he spent a lot of time along the wharves, associating with "blackguard sailor boys." From them, he picked up a habit of uncontrollable swearing and a proclivity for fighting that often got him into trouble.

William went to Scotland for education when he was ten. He spent two years at a preparatory school in Dumfries and a year at Edinburgh University, before returning to Charleston to begin a medical apprenticeship under Dr. Alexander Garden. He planned to return to Edinburgh to study medicine, but the beginning of the revolution hastened his departure. Liberty Boys pressured him to sign the Association. He refused to subscribe to what he considered an act of rebellion. With his mother's blessing, he joined his father in London. He began medical studies at Edinburgh later that year. In the autumn of 1778, he left before receiving his medical degree. He returned to London to study anatomy and surgery with the renowned William Hunter. After a brief stint as a surgeon in a Scottish regiment in the Netherlands, which nearly ended in a duel, he enrolled at Leiden University. He wrote a medical thesis there for which Edinburgh University awarded him the MD in 1780. He was ready to begin the practice of medicine in London when the revolution disrupted his life again. After the British captured Charleston, his father asked him to return there to manage the family's affairs. Robert was unhappy with John's conduct.

Shortly before leaving for Carolina, William learned that the British had captured and imprisoned Henry Laurens. He knew Laurens and his family well. Before sailing, William wrote "An Account of Mr. Henry Laurens," which was published in *The Public Advertiser*. He described Laurens as a man of good character and urged the British government to treat him well. William arrived in Charleston in January 1781, expecting to find his brother John a British prisoner. Instead, John was wearing the uniform of a captain in the Loyalist militia. He had managed another timely political transformation and placed the family newspaper at the service of the British military administration. After March 1781, the newspaper sported a new title: *The Royal Gazette*. The Wells brothers ran it together for several months before John went to London to patch up relations with his father. William became a captain in the Loyalist militia as well as running the printing business and dealing with his father's legal matters. The commandant of Charleston, Lieutenant Colonel Nisbet Balfour, asked William to write and publish a warning to men who had sworn allegiance to the Crown after the surrender. Loyalist militia were deserting, many of them joining the rebels. The notice stated that such conduct was treasonable and liable to the punishment of death. Balfour later used the warning to justify the execution of Colonel Isaac Hayne. In his memoir, William expressed regret for having published the notice. He published a more conciliatory piece in August 1782, when he learned that his boyhood friend John Laurens had been killed in a skirmish near Charleston. The war was all but over, and the British were preparing to evacuate Charleston. William wrote an obituary of John remarkable for its homage to a fallen enemy:

> *John Laurens' generosity of temper and liberality of opinion were as extensive as his abilities. The only blemish in his character is his decision to rebel against his king. While we are marking the death of an enemy who was dangerous to our cause from his abilities, we hope we shall stand excused for paying tribute to the moral excellences of his character. Happy would it be for the distressed families who are to leave this garrison with His Majesty's troops, that another John Laurens could be found.*

William probably knew that John had advocated lenient treatment of Loyalists at Jacksonborough. When the British evacuated Charleston in December 1782, William left on a ship going to St. Augustine. He disassembled a printing press, took it with him, reassembled it and established the first weekly newspaper in Florida, *The East Florida Gazette*.

In the summer of 1783, after peace had been declared, William returned to Charleston for the last time. Robert asked him to go there to recover unpaid debts. William went reluctantly. Tensions between Loyalists and Americans remained high. He entered the city under a flag of truce. It was as if he had aroused a hornet's nest. Many Whites were furious at the British refusal to return runaway slaves to their owners. William was personally obnoxious to people who remembered his support for the British. The sheriff of Charleston arrested him regarding a transaction John had made and sent him to jail. The sheriff told William he would release him once the British returned the runaways. He published a justification for the arrest in which he called Wells "a sinner of the first magnitude" who had committed "high crimes and misdemeanours." William protested that his only crime had been to love his country, meaning Britain.

Charleston at the end of the war was a disorderly, almost anarchic place. A couple who offered William hospitality, John and Elizabeth Harleston, were rewarded by having a mob attack their house. The same night, a mob dragged another recent British arrival, a lawyer, from his residence and threw him into the river. His crime was to be the son of James Simpson, a Loyalist and former royal attorney general of South Carolina. William spent three months in a leaky jail cell before a British commissioner secured his freedom. The commissioner convinced a reluctant William to pay "an unjust demand" for money, after which the sheriff released him. He returned to St. Augustine, but not without another hair-raising adventure. Leaving Charleston Harbor, his ship ran aground on the bar. Pounded by large waves, the vessel seemed about to break up. William took off his clothes and tied himself to the capstan to prevent being washed into the sea. After a while, the weather moderated, and the ship remained intact. With night coming on, the passengers who could swim began to jump into the sea and make their way across the bar to deeper water, where rescue boats were waiting. William, a poor swimmer, decided to take his chances and follow them. With the help of a sailor, he made it to the boats and safety. The next day, the ship broke into pieces.

William did not stay long in St. Augustine. As part of the peace treaty of 1783, Britain ceded Florida back to Spain. He had spent more than three years in America dealing with the consequences of the war. From Florida, he went to London, where he finally opened a medical practice in 1785, but the war's effects hindered him even in that. His father had made some bad loans. He had fallen into debt and was unable to help William with the expenses of establishing himself as a physician. Robert applied for compensation from the Loyalist Claims Commission for his losses in America. He eventually received some money, but the amount was too small to cover his debts. In 1791, a stroke disabled him. He died three years later, still in debt. Instead of receiving help from his family, William had to help his mother and his sisters Helena and Priscilla, who had established a school for girls in London. He could not afford to buy a carriage, a virtual necessity for a London physician hoping to attract wealthy patients. Humiliatingly, he had to visit patients on foot. He never secured many private patients or a sizeable income and amassed debts from borrowing money from wealthier colleagues. He managed to secure a prestigious post as senior physician at St. Thomas' Hospital in 1800, but soon afterward he suffered a mild stroke. He was unable to work for months and suffered some memory loss. He adopted a vegetarian diet and never had another attack, but his health began a slow decline.

His mind remained sharp. Before and after the stroke, he made important contributions to medical and scientific research. He also fought a long and futile battle trying to force London's Royal College of Physicians to open its fellowship to doctors from all recognized universities. At the time, it was restricted almost entirely to graduates of Oxford and Cambridge, who benefited financially from the prestige of having FRCP after their names. William presented and published dozens of medical and scientific papers. One of his scientific works, *An Essay Upon Single Vision with Two Eyes* (1792), anticipated the conclusions of modern research. It gained him membership in the Royal Society. In 1814, the society awarded him its Rumford Medal for his *Essay on Dew.* Victorian scientists Sir John Herschel and John Tyndall praised the essay as a model of inductive method. The year before he won the medal, Wells had presented a paper to the society that attracted little attention at the time. In it, he stated the principle of natural selection, forty-six years before Darwin published *The Origin of Species*. Darwin was unaware of Wells's paper at the time, but in later editions he acknowledged that William Wells was probably the first person to state the principle. William never followed up on that work. His health continued to worsen. He died of congestive heart failure in 1817 and was buried next to his parents at St. Bride's Fleet Street, then known as the Printers' Church. War disturbed him even there when German bombs struck the church in 1940.

# BOSTON KING

When the British attacked Charleston in the spring of 1780, thousands of enslaved Africans fled to the British lines. Sir Henry Clinton's proclamation promising them freedom sparked a mass exodus from the plantations. The runaways included a young man named Boston King, who produced one of the few accounts of the revolution by a former slave. King was born on a plantation near Charleston owned by Richard Waring, around 1760. His father, who was literate, had been "stolen away into slavery when he was young." Waring had been on good terms with his father and his mother, a skilled herbalist, and treated them well. Boston's experience was less fortunate. As a boy, he trained as a house servant. When he was sixteen, Waring apprenticed him to a carpenter, who beat him "without mercy." Learning about the abuse, Waring terminated the apprenticeship. Around that time, the British had begun their siege of Charleston. Waring took King into the country to prevent British soldiers from seizing him. After they captured the city, King fled there to escape another severe beating at the hands of an angry White man and to gain his liberty.

When he arrived in Charleston, the British welcomed him: "I began to feel the happiness of liberty, of which I knew nothing before." His elation was soon tempered by harsh reality. The arrival of thousands of the enslaved overwhelmed the ability or willingness of the British authorities to cope. The runaways often lacked basic food, medicine, clothing and shelter. Smallpox and a mysterious fever spread among them with

*A Black Wood Cutter at Shelburne, Nova Scotia*, 1780s. *Library and Archives of Canada.*

terrifying rapidity. King contracted smallpox. The authorities removed the infected to the racecourse about a mile north of Charleston. There, they lay in the open without adequate food or care. A British soldier nursed and fed King, and he recovered. He was later able to return the kindness when his benefactor was wounded in battle. While serving with the British, King narrowly avoided being sold back into slavery on several occasions. In one episode, a Loyalist officer, Captain Lewes, intended to sell him. King discovered that Lewes was stealing horses from the British army and was about to switch allegiance to the rebel side. King escaped and alerted Lewes's British superior to his plan. In the following months, King later performed the dangerous task of carrying dispatches through enemy lines. One message he carried while stationed at Nelson's Ferry (near Eutawville) helped save 250 soldiers from being captured by the Americans. He later joined the crew of a British man-of-war and took part in the capture of a rebel ship in Chesapeake Bay. His ship went to New York City with its prize. New York was the most important British stronghold in the former colonies, and King decided to stay there. He worked at various jobs, including crew member on a pilot boat. An American ship captured his, and King was once more nearly forced back into slavery. He escaped again and returned to New York. By then, the war was nearly over. The British had already evacuated Georgia and the Carolinas. They had brought thousands of Black Loyalists to New York. King met and married a former slave from North Carolina named Violet. Most Whites were jubilant when peace was announced, but for Blacks who had taken refuge with the British the end of the war brought a renewed threat of re-enslavement. Rumors circulated that the runaways would be returned to their White masters, as stipulated in the Treaty of Paris. Slave owners were arriving in the city and seizing their former slaves. The news filled King and his friends with "anguish and terror." They were saved when the British commander in America, Sir Guy Carleton, refused to implement Article 7. Carleton argued that Black Loyalists were no longer property but free persons. Returning them to slavery would violate British promises. His decision not only angered Americans but also infuriated many Loyalist slave owners and unscrupulous traders who hoped to profit from returning the Blacks to their owners. Carleton shipped them to Nova Scotia, where many White Loyalists were also taking refuge. In all, the British gave certificates of freedom to more than five thousand Black Loyalists.

In Nova Scotia, Boston and Violet helped to establish a Black Loyalist settlement, Birchtown. They named the town in honor of General Samuel Birch, the British commandant in New York City who had organized the evacuation of the Black Loyalists. King worked at various jobs to support himself. He converted to Methodism and became a circuit riding preacher. Life in sparsely populated Nova Scotia was hard. The difficulties were increased by poor soil and a harsh climate. Tensions with White neighbors were often high as both communities competed for scarce resources and jobs. Many of the Whites were southern Loyalists who had brought slaves with them. In 1792, the Kings accepted an offer from the new Sierra Leone Company to help establish a colony in West Africa for freed slaves. The Kings recruited hundreds of other Blacks in Nova Scotia to join the exodus. Some of them came from South Carolina. Isaac Anderson was a carpenter, born a freeman. Cato Perkins had been a slave in Charleston.

The company's backers were British antislavery leaders. They included Granville Sharp, William Wilberforce and brothers Thomas and John Clarkson. Led by John Clarkson, King, his wife and about 1,100 other settlers immigrated to the new colony. They established the settlement of Freetown, Sierra Leone's capital today. Tragically, Violet died soon after their arrival, probably of yellow fever. Many other new arrivals, both White and Black, also died. The Sierra Leone Company employed King to preach to the Indigenous people. The task proved immensely difficult because he did not understand their languages. He proposed to open a school to teach English. In 1794, the company sent him to Kingswood School, a Methodist institution near Bristol. He trained as a missionary and teacher before returning to Sierra Leone in 1796. While at Kingswood, he wrote his autobiography, which the *Methodist Magazine* published in 1798. It is one of few accounts written by a Black Loyalist. After his return, he remarried. His second wife, Peggy, relocated with him about one hundred miles inland to missionize among the Sherbo people. Both died there in 1802, probably of yellow fever. Indigenous rulers viewed the new settlement as a threat to their territory and attacked Freetown several times. The company's forces defeated them and made them sign away their sovereignty. In 1808, the company went bankrupt. The British government took over the administration of Sierra Leone, adding it to the empire. The settlers who had fled slavery in America gained a kind of freedom but as subjects to new masters in London.

# DAVID RAMSAY

David Ramsay was an active participant in and a major early historian of the American Revolution. He was born in Lancaster County, Pennsylvania, in 1749, son of Scottish or Scotch-Irish emigrants. He graduated from The College of New Jersey (now Princeton University) in 1765. In 1773, Ramsay became one of the first recipients of the MD degree from the College of Philadelphia (now the University of Pennsylvania). Ramsay moved to Charleston, South Carolina, the following year on the recommendation of his mentor, Dr. Benjamin Rush. After a slow start, Ramsay built a lucrative medical practice. When the revolution began, he joined the Whigs. During the war, he served in the state assembly and the governor's council and as an army surgeon. The British exiled him to St. Augustine after the surrender of Charleston, along with Gadsden and about twenty others. Released the following year, he went to Philadelphia, where he became a member of the Continental Congress. He served in that body until 1786, after which he

David Ramsay, by Charles Wilson Peale, 1770s. *U.S. National Portrait Gallery*.

returned to South Carolina. During the 1790s, voters elected Ramsay to the state senate on several occasions. He ran unsuccessfully for the U.S. Senate. His opponent, using a tactic that would become common in South Carolina, accused him of being insufficiently supportive of slavery.

Ramsay came to Charleston as an opponent of slavery, as was Rush. His opinions shifted gradually during the following years. Without endorsing slavery, he found ways to justify it as "a necessary evil." In 1780, he wrote to Rush that living in South Carolina had convinced him that God had designed Blacks for labor in hot, humid and sickly South Carolina: "Providence intended this for a Negro settlement. Their constitution is undoubtedly better suited to the climate, and all planters tell us that their lands cannot be cultivated by white men." The phrase "all planters tell us" is revealing. It indicates that Ramsay was absorbing the local White elite culture. One of the planters who influenced him was undoubtedly Henry Laurens. In 1787, Ramsay married Laurens's daughter Martha, who had been in France during the Revolutionary War. She was Ramsay's third wife. The first two, Sabina Ellis and Frances Witherspoon, had died within a year of their weddings. Through his marriage to Martha Laurens, Ramsay became connected to some of the wealthiest and most powerful planting families in South Carolina. Despite his connections, he experienced financial problems and declared bankruptcy in the 1790s. After the revolution, he devoted much of his time to writing. He wrote several medical and historical works. The medical writings are largely derivative and influenced by Rush's "heroic" medicine, which recommended heavy bleeding and strong purging for most ailments. The heroic regime was hardly a medical advance. It sent many a sufferer to an early grave. More positively, Ramsay was a pioneer in promoting the use of Edward Jenner's cowpox vaccine for smallpox, which soon replaced the riskier inoculation. Ramsay began vaccinating as early as 1802. He predicted that a general use of the technique could eliminate smallpox from the world. He was right, although the goal was not achieved until the late 1970s.

It is for his historical works, not his political or medical labors, that Ramsay is best known today. He wrote some of the earliest histories of the American Revolution, works in which he took an increasingly nationalist and conservative position. In 1785, he published a detailed *History of the Revolution of South Carolina*. It describes many events he was witness to or a participant in. He followed with *History of the American Revolution* (1789) and *History of South Carolina* (1809). A *History of the United States* appeared in 1816–17,

David Ramsay's house on Broad Street, Charleston. *Author's collection.*

shortly after his death, which was sudden and violent. In 1815, Charleston authorities asked him to examine tailor William Linnen, who had attempted to murder his lawyer. Ramsay concluded that Linnen was not guilty of a crime because he was insane. In making this claim, Ramsay aligned himself with medical ideas that were not yet widely accepted. He had also advocated the creation of a state asylum for the insane. After Linnen appeared to have regained his sanity, the authorities released him. He threatened Ramsay for calling him a lunatic, but Ramsay did not take the threat seriously. On May 6, 1815, Linnen walked up to Ramsay on Broad Street, pulled out a pistol and shot him at close range. Shocked onlookers carried Ramsay to his nearby home. He died two days later, insisting to the last that Linnen was "a lunatic free from guilt." Ramsay was buried in Charleston's Circular Congregational Church on Meeting Street.

# ISAAC HAYNE

As the year 1779 opened, the question of allegiance to the state of South Carolina assumed new urgency. The British had just seized Savannah. Their commander, Colonel Archibald Campbell, published a proclamation urging Americans to return to their allegiance to the Crown. South Carolina's assembly responded with a new law that made attempting to join the British a crime punishable by death. William Tweed and Andrew Groundwater were hanged under the new law in Charleston on March 15. They were apprehended trying to take a message to Colonel Campbell. They were also suspected of arson. During the War for Independence, both sides executed captured soldiers and civilians. Some received a trial of sorts; most did not. Most of the executions were essentially lynchings. At King's Mountain in October 1780, the victorious rebels killed defeated Loyalists after they had surrendered. King's Mountain was part of a broader pattern of tit-for-tat killings that plagued the backcountry during the British occupation of 1780–82. At King's Mountain, the victors yelled "Tarleton's Quarter!" as they shot the Loyalists. The cry referred to an incident during the Battle of Waxhaws in late May. The British Legion, a Loyalist force commanded by Lieutenant Colonel Banastre Tarleton, shot some of the Continentals after they had surrendered. American accounts called it a massacre and claimed Tarleton had refused them quarter. British and Loyalist accounts countered that Tarleton did not deny quarter and stopped the shooting as quickly as he could. Whatever the truth, "Tarleton's Quarter" came to mean "No Quarter." After the shootings ended at King's Mountain, the victors hanged nine Loyalist prisoners following a mock trial. They intended to hang about twenty more but fled when they learned that Tarleton's Legion was approaching. In May 1781, Whig militia captain Joseph McCord ordered the summary execution of fourteen captured Loyalist prisoners. Loyalist "Bloody Bill" Cunningham became infamous for butchering Whigs and their families. On one occasion, his band slaughtered almost thirty drunken Whigs they stumbled upon. Both sides accused the other of dismembering captives. Governor John Rutledge ordered partisan leaders Thomas Sumter and Francis Marion to hang "renegade Negroes," Blacks who had helped the British. How many Black people the partisans executed is unknown. Most of the victims of these war crimes, Black or White, were anonymous or, at most, names on a list. Few of their names are etched in historical memory. An exception is Nathan Hale of Connecticut. The British hanged him as a spy in 1776. He is remembered for his alleged last words: "I regret that I have but one life to give for my country."

Isaac Hayne is less well-known than Hale, but he was the most famous person the British executed in the southern colonies during the war. A painting of Hayne being led from the Provost Dungeon to his execution hangs in the Fireproof Building, the headquarters of the South Carolina Historical Society. Thomas Jeremiah might compete with Hayne for recognition in some quarters today, but he was forgotten until recently. Hayne and Jeremiah had little in common besides being hanged, but they did share one other thing. They were sacrificial lambs. They were not the only ones, just the most famous. Who remembers Colonel Hamilton Ballendine? Newspaper reports mention that General Lincoln ordered Ballendine summarily executed as a spy on March 5, 1780. A picket guard Lincoln had sent to the Stono River seized him on his way to the enemy. They found drawings of Charleston's defensive works in his pocket. The reports do not mention if Ballendine was a rebel turncoat or a Loyalist or if he said anything before being hanged. Many others who shared his fate are nameless.

The British charged Hayne with treason, a charge he vigorously disputed. How he got into that situation is a convoluted story, and contemporary accounts vary. Hayne owned several plantations near Jacksonborough, about thirty miles south of Charleston. He served as a cavalry officer in the South Carolina militia. After the fall of Charleston in May 1780, the British paroled him. He returned to his home at Hayne Hall. The

*The Execution of Isaac Hayne* by Caroll N. Jones. *Permission, South Carolina Historical Society.*

victor, Sir Henry Clinton, went back to New York in June, but before he left, he issued three proclamations designed to restore order and royal government in South Carolina. One promised a full pardon to rebels who would resume their allegiance to the British Crown. That was the carrot. There was also a stick. Persons who refused the oath would be liable to severe punishment and confiscation of estates. The third proclamation affected men like Hayne who had been paroled. It freed them from their paroles and restored their rights as loyal subjects of the king. That might seem an attractive option. But as "loyal subjects" they had a duty to help restore order, and that might include serving in the Loyalist militia against their former comrades. If they failed to sign the oath of allegiance to the Crown, they would be treated as rebels and their property would be subject to confiscation. In effect, Clinton was forcing them to choose a side. Many of them viewed the proclamations as a violation of the terms of surrender and joined the rebels. The man Clinton left in command in South Carolina, Lord Cornwallis, believed the proclamations were a mistake that would make his job harder. They did.

Before Hayne could decide what to do, smallpox struck his family in Colleton County. One of his children died of it, and his wife and two other children became infected. A Loyalist officer who knew Hayne advised him to go to Charleston and submit. He went, but it is reasonable to conclude that he was in a distraught and confused state of mind. He rode to Charleston. He went to see Dr. David Ramsay for political and medical advice. The British commandant at the time, General James Paterson, arrested Hayne while he was in town. Paterson threatened to imprison Hayne if he refused to sign the oath of allegiance to the Crown. Desperate to get home to his sick family, he agreed to sign after Paterson assured him, he claimed, that he would not be required to take up arms against his former comrades. During Hayne's absence, his wife died from smallpox.

When the Whigs regained control of most of the state in the spring of 1781, Hayne concluded that he no longer owed allegiance to Britain. He joined the partisans. In July, he took part in a raid designed to kidnap—or possibly free—Andrew Williamson, a former Whig general. Williamson was either a southern Benedict Arnold or an American spy. A British detachment led by Major Archibald Campbell caught up with the partisans and released Williamson. Campbell captured Hayne and took him back to Charleston as a prisoner. By then, Lieutenant Colonel Nisbet Balfour had replaced Paterson as commandant of the city. Balfour was a veteran of the war who was wounded at Bunker Hill and fought in several other battles.

He imprisoned Hayne in the Provost Dungeon, the bottom floor of the Exchange. He charged Hayne with treason for having rejoined the rebels in violation of his oath of allegiance to the Crown. Before proceeding further, Balfour awaited the return to Charleston of his nominal superior, Francis, Lord Rawdon. Like Balfour, Rawdon had been in America since the start of the rebellion, and like him, believed that harsh methods were required to defeat it.

Hayne expected to receive a formal trial. Rawdon and Balfour decided they could not risk a civilian trial. Hayne was a popular and respected figure in Charleston. They could not court-martial him either because he was not a British officer. They convened a board of inquiry composed of several officers who interrogated Hayne. Based on their report, Rawdon and Balfour declared Hayne guilty of treason and sentenced him to hang. To justify the lack of a trial, they later claimed that Hayne was a spy as well as a traitor. They had another motive: revenge. The previous October, Americans had hanged British Major John André as a spy at Tappan, New York. André was captured returning to British lines after a secret meeting with Benedict Arnold, to arrange Arnold's switch to the British side. The Americans had used a board of inquiry, of which Nathanael Greene was a member, to condemn André to death. Washington approved the death sentence. André was an amiable, talented and popular officer. Balfour was his close friend. Rawdon had trained André to replace him as adjutant general in New York. The British officers were not the only ones seeking revenge. For months, Loyalists had been streaming into Charleston, bringing tales of rebel atrocities and demanding retribution. British officers accused Hayne of committing "acts of brutality" against a convoy of wounded redcoats. Rawdon and Balfour cited instances of cruelty inflicted on Loyalist officers as a justification for Hayne's sentence.

Hayne protested the proceeding and verdict. He claimed to believe the board of inquiry was preliminary to a trial and that he would have called witnesses and requested legal counsel had he known it was not. Many prominent Charlestonians urged the British officers to reconsider the death sentence. They included Loyalists. One of them was William Bull, the last royal lieutenant governor. Bull had returned from England in 1781 to serve as head of the civilian administration, the Board of Police. According to one narrative, Bull was unable to walk, and slaves carried him in a litter before the British commanders. Balfour responded curtly to Bull's request with "Remember André." Women from both sides pleaded for mercy. At play here was a complicated web of intermarriage and interdependence among the Charleston elite that cut across nominal political divisions. One of the petitioners was Mary Peronneau, sister of Hayne's deceased wife. She was also the sister-in-law of Alexander Garden's wife, Elizabeth. Mary famously brought two of Hayne's children before Rawdon and begged him for a reprieve on her knees. Some British officers also petitioned on Hayne's behalf, including the man who captured him, Major Archibald Campbell. Rawdon and Balfour refused all the appeals for mercy. Their only concession was to allow Hayne a stay of several days to see his children. They refused his request to be executed by firing squad rather than hanged. Major Campbell is alleged to have said that he would have shot Hayne on the spot if he had known that hanging would be his fate. Ironically, partisans captured Campbell a few months later and shot him, claiming he was trying to escape.

At dawn on August 4, Hayne's captors led him out of the Provost Dungeon. Several hundred soldiers escorted him to the place of execution at Boundary Street, close to the present-day College of Charleston. An old, perhaps apocryphal story relates that Mary Peronneau called out to him from her window as Hayne walked by, "Return, return to us, dear Isaac." He replied, "I will, if I can." Because this is Charleston, Hayne, or his ghost, returned to haunt the house. Hayne's execution elevated him to the status of a martyr to the American cause in South Carolina. He became a figure in southern folklore, celebrated in story, song, poetry and art. National histories largely ignored him, especially after the Civil War, as they largely ignored the savage struggle that took place in South Carolina during the last stages of the war.

Immediately after Hayne was executed, Rawdon applied to leave for England. He cited poor health and exhaustion after two years of campaigning in feverish South Carolina. Fear of retaliation may have sped up his departure. He asked Dr. Alexander Garden for a medical certificate to validate his request to leave. Garden refused. He was angry because Rawdon was leaving at such a critical time and had refused to pardon Hayne. Rawdon found another doctor, who issued a certificate, and left. On the voyage home, a French ship captured his. When he finally reached England early in 1782, he discovered that some British politicians were claiming that Hayne's execution was unjustified and were blaming him. The Duke of Richmond, an opponent of the American war, moved to censure Rawdon in the House of Lords. The peers voted against Richmond's motion, but Rawdon demanded the duke make an apology or face him on the field of honor. A duel was narrowly avoided when Richmond issued an apology. Rawdon went on to become governor-general of India and racked up several peerages. In later years, he tried to shift responsibility for Hayne's execution to Balfour. In a letter to Henry Lee in 1813, Rawdon claimed he had urged mercy, that it was Balfour who insisted on hanging Hayne. Rawdon's argument was convoluted, unconvincing and contradictory. Balfour never had a chance to respond to it. The letter was not published until 1824, the year after Balfour died. A few years earlier, however, Balfour had told some dinner guests that he was willing to consider leniency and that it was Rawdon who refused. Balfour bore the brunt of local anger for the execution after Rawdon left Charleston. In his memoirs, General William Moultrie denounced Balfour as a "haughty Scot" of "tyrannical disposition" who treated people like slaves. It was an ironic statement, given that Moultrie's father had been born in Scotland and Moultrie was a slaveholder. In March 1782, General Leslie, who replaced Rawdon as British commander in South Carolina, informed Clinton that Balfour's situation was "very unpleasant" and his life in danger. Leslie sent Balfour to New York a few months later. Balfour eventually rose to the rank of major general. He served during the wars against France in the 1790s and in Parliament.

After learning of Hayne's execution, the South Carolina delegation in the Continental Congress moved that General Washington should be ordered to hang a captured British officer of similar rank. They demanded it as retaliation for Hayne's "murder." The motion failed, but it illustrates the cycle of revenge that had gripped South Carolina. Instead, Congress instructed General Nathanael Greene to investigate the circumstances of Hayne's execution and, if he found it violated the laws of war, to execute a British officer. Greene wrote to Balfour, asking him to explain why Hayne was hanged. Balfour replied that he was following orders laid down by his superior, Lord Cornwallis. That was not strictly true. Cornwallis had directed that militia who had fought with the British and then joined the rebels should be executed. Hayne had never fought with the British and thus did not come under Cornwallis's order. When Greene threatened to hang a British officer, Balfour responded that such an action might trigger a cycle of executions. Greene disputed Balfour's reasoning but never carried out his threat. After Cornwallis surrendered at Yorktown, South Carolina delegates in Congress moved that Washington hang him. Arthur Middleton presented the motion. The motion failed by a slim majority. Opponents argued that executing Cornwallis would violate the terms of surrender agreed to at Yorktown and place a stain on Washington's honor. They might have added that it would likely prolong the war due to British anger. In the end, Cornwallis was exchanged for Henry Laurens. Peace negotiations opened in Paris shortly thereafter.

# EPILOGUE

## *History Is Messy*

The British evacuated Charleston on December 14, 1782. Hardly anyone remembers that date now, but for many years, Charlestonians celebrated December 14 as a holiday, Victory Day. Surprisingly, no beer company has tried to revive it. On the surface, the evacuation was remarkably peaceful, even dignified. By prior agreement between the commanders on both sides, American soldiers did not enter the city until the ships were ready to depart. The last to board the transports were British and Loyalist soldiers, who marched from their lines at Boundary Street to the wharves, followed by a detachment of Continentals. The two forces were separated by a few hundred yards, but not a shot was fired. Whites who remained in the city cheered the entering army as heroes. Many of them had likely cheered the British when they arrived two and a half years before. The last British commander in the South, General Alexander Leslie, inherited the thankless task of organizing the withdrawal. It was an enormous headache. His greatest desire was to get away from Charleston as soon as possible. His conversation was largely limited to the unbearable heat, the "damn fevers" and the daughter he had not seen for several years. Leslie's negotiations—with Greene, with White Loyalists and with Americans demanding he leave their runaway slaves behind—had been trying. Loyalists were furious about being abandoned and losing their property, real and human. They viewed the British withdrawal as a betrayal. For them, the voyage ahead and the life beyond produced much anxiety. But at least they could feel secure in their personal freedom. The thousands of Blacks who had put their trust in the British could not be sure even of that.

Historians estimate that about twenty-five thousand slaves fled South Carolina plantations during the war, more than one-fifth of the entire Black population. Some found freedom. Some died of disease or violence. Others ended up enslaved again in the West Indies or in the new United States. The British promised to free slaves who entered their lines, but these were not guarantees of liberty. Boston King escaped being forced back into slavery several times. Many others were less lucky than he. More than seven thousand Blacks received permission to leave Charleston with the British. Untold numbers did not. The most tragic moment of the evacuation occurred when Blacks who had not received permission clung to the boats taking those who did to the transport ships. Others, desperate to avoid returning to American masters they feared would punish them severely, had signed on with merchants who cynically resold them to West Indian planters.

The population of Charleston in 1783 differed considerably from that in 1775. Emigration and mortality had reduced and altered the population. Blacks ceased to be the majority in the city and state, although slave imports during the next two decades would reverse that trend. The White population grew more quickly at first through immigration and natural increase, but by 1820 Black people were once again a majority. Many White Loyalists had left voluntarily or were banished. Their numbers included planters, merchants, doctors and political leaders. Several of them had made or would make important contributions to science and culture. Alexander Garden was one of the leading naturalists of colonial America. After the war, his pupil William Charles Wells undertook significant scientific research and became the first person to propose the theory of natural selection. His sister Helena Wells wrote two novels and two books on issues relating to women's education after her family went to Britain. Their father, Robert, was an innovative bookseller and printer and a vigorous promoter of culture in Charleston.

History is often unpleasant, messy and chaotic. Historical myth is the opposite: neat, generally pleasing—at least to our prejudices—and comfortably black and white. The myths are "alternative facts"—fake history. The comforting myths and legends that constitute public memory tend to dominate if not obliterate actual history in the popular consciousness. By *actual history* I do not mean the truth but the result of painstaking historical research, writing and interpretation. Done well, the result is our best approximation of the truth. In that sense, history resembles science. Science is a more exact business, of course. Scientists can use repeated experiments to confirm their hypotheses. Historians do not have that luxury. They cannot repeat historical events. The writing of history is "not a visit of condolence" as Sir Lewis Namier put it. The same is true of reading it. Learning our history is often troubling and confusing. If it never is, we are reading the wrong stuff. Some people avoid the trouble by ignoring history. Henry Ford supposedly said that "history is bunk." He may not have said exactly that, but he did reject the past as dead and meaningless, not worth bothering about. Abraham Lincoln disagreed. In his Second Inaugural Address, he declared, "My Fellow Americans, we cannot escape history." He understood that the terrible war nearing its end in 1865 was the result of the country's failure to abolish slavery early in its history. Novelist William Faulkner held a similar view: "The past isn't dead. It is not even past." His characters are prisoners of their history. Karl Marx wrote in much the same vein in *The Eighteenth Brumaire of Louis Bonaparte* (1852):

> *Men make their own history, but they do not make it as they please; they do not make it under self-selected circumstances, but under circumstances existing already, given and transmitted from the past. The tradition of all dead generations weighs like a nightmare on the brains of the living.*

One does not have to be a Marxist to agree with that. Our history, like our biology, constrains us, for good or ill. Shortly before Henry Laurens came to Paris in November 1782, a renowned artist had come to paint the peace delegations for posterity. Benjamin West was American born, a Pennsylvanian who settled in England in 1763. He earned recognition for his paintings of historic subjects. He is perhaps best known for *The Death of General Wolfe*. West's treaty painting was never completed. The American delegation is pictured, but Henry Laurens, in red at the back, is only partially finished. Was that because Laurens arrived so late? Perhaps, but the British delegation is not in the painting at all. West intended to put them where the blank space is on the right. He never did because they refused to sit for him. The unfinished painting ended up in John Adams's possession. It remained in the Adams family for many years. It currently hangs in the Winterthur Museum in Delaware. The treaty painting inadvertently sums up much about the American War for Independence: a revolution proclaiming lofty ideals it failed to

*Treaty of Paris* by Benjamin West, unfinished, 1782. *Courtesy Winterthur Museum.*

achieve. In that sense it is fitting that Henry Laurens, who proclaimed his abhorrence of slavery but took no action against it, should be portrayed as half present, half absent.

# BIBLIOGRAPHY

## *Primary Sources*

Aikman, Louisa Wells. *The Journal of a Voyage from Charlestown, S.C., to London*. New York Historical Society, 1906.

American Loyalist Claims Commission: Records, National Archives, Kew. AO12/46-52, T79

Colonial Office Papers, National Archives, Kew CO5.

Cornwallis Papers, National Archives, Kew PRO 30/11.

Drayton, John. *Memoirs of the American Revolution*. 2 vols., Charleston, 1821. Based on documents John's father, William Henry Drayton, had collected.

Gibbes, R.W. *Documentary History of the American Revolution*. 3 vols. New York: 1855–57.

Guy Carleton, 1st Baron Dorchester, Papers, National Archives, Kew PRO 30/55.

Journal of the Council of Safety for the Province of South-Carolina, 1775. Collections of the South Carolina Historical Society, vol. 2, 22–24.

Journal of the Second Council of Safety, appointed by the Provincial Congress, November 1775, Collections of the South Carolina Historical Society, vol. 3, 35–271.

King, Boston. "Memoirs of the Life of Boston King, A Black Preacher." *Methodist Magazine*, 1798. Republished in *The Life of Boston King, Black Loyalist, Minister, and Master Carpenter*, edited by Ruth Holmes Whitehead and Carmelita A.M. Robertson, Nimbus Publishing Limited & The Nova Scotia Museum, 2003.

Laurens, Henry. *The Papers of Henry Laurens.* 16 vols. University of South Carolina Press, 1972–2003.

Milligen, George. *A Short Description of the Province of South-Carolina, With an Account of the Air, Water, and Diseases at Charles-Town. Written in the Year 1763.* London, 1770.

Moultrie, William. *Memoirs of the American Revolution So Far as It Related to the States of South Carolina, North Carolina, and Georgia*. New York, 1802.

Papers of the First Council of Safety of the Revolutionary Party in South Carolina, June–November 1775. *The South Carolina Historical and Genealogical Magazine*. Vols. 2–4, 1901–03.

Ramsay, David. *The History of the Revolution in South Carolina*. Trenton, NJ, 1785.

Report by George Milligen, Surgeon to the Garrison for His Majesty's Forces in South Carolina, dated 15 September 1775. National Archives, Kew CO5 396 037._

*Royal Gazette*, 1781–82.

Smith, James Edward. *A Selection of the Correspondence of Linnaeus and Other Naturalists*. 2 vols., London, 1821.

*South Carolina and American General Gazette*, 1765–81.

*South Carolina Gazette*, 1765–75.

*A South Carolina Protest Against Slavery: Being a Letter from Henry Laurens, Second President of the Continental Congress, to His Son, Colonel John Laurens; Dated Charleston, S C., August 14th, 1776*. G.P. Putnam, 1861.

Wells, William Charles. *Two Essays: Upon a Single Vision with Two Eyes, the Other on Dew*. London, 1818. This volume contains Wells's memoir of his life and the essay in which he proposes the idea of natural selection.

## *Secondary Sources*

Berkeley, Edmund, and Dorothy Smith Berkeley. *Dr. Alexander Garden of Charles Town*. University of North Carolina Press, 1969.

Bicheno, Hugh. *Rebels and Redcoats: The American Revolutionary War*. Harper Collins, 2003.

Blumrosen, Alfred W. and Ruth G. Blumrosen. *Slave Nation: How Slavery United the Colonies and Sparked the American Revolution.* Source Books, 2005.

Borick, Carl P. *A Gallant Defense: The Siege of Charleston, 1780*. University of South Carolina Press, 2003.

Bowden, David K. *The Execution of Isaac Hayne.* Sandlapper Store, 1977.

Bragg, C.L. *Martyr of the American Revolution: The Execution of Isaac Hayne, South Carolinian.* University of South Carolina Press, 2016.

Butler, Nicholas. "The Charleston Tar-and-Feathers Incident of 1775." Charleston County Public Library. https://www.ccpl.org.

Calhoon, Robert M., *The Loyalists in Revolutionary America.* Harcourt Brace Jovanovich, 1973.

Calhoon, Robert M. and Robert M. Weir. "The Scandalous History of Sir Edgerton Leigh." In *Tory Insurgents: The Loyalist Perception and Other Essays*, edited by Robert M. Calhoon and Timothy M. Barnes. University of South Carolina Press, 2012.

Calloway, Colin G. *The American Revolution in Indian Country: Crisis and Diversity in Native American Communities.* Cambridge University Press, 1995.

Coclanis, Peter A. *The Shadow of a Dream: Economic Life and Death in the South Carolina Low Country 1670–1920.* Oxford University Press, 1989.

Colley, Linda. *Britons: Forging the Nation, 1707–1837.* Yale University Press, 1992.

Dabney, William, and Marion Dargan. *William Henry Drayton and the American Revolution.* University of New Mexico Press, 1962.

David, Huw. "James Crokatt's 'Exceeding Good Counting House': Ascendancy and Influence in the Transatlantic Carolina Trade." *South Carolina Historical Magazine*, 111, nos. 3-4 (July–October 2010): 151–74.

Edgar, Walter. *Partisans and Redcoats: The Southern Conflict That Turned the Tide of the American Revolution.* Harper Collins, 2001.

Edgar, Walter B., ed. *The South Carolina Encyclopedia*, digital edition, expanded from print edition. University of South Carolina Press, 2006.

Eldridge, Kelcey. "A Forgotten Founder: The Life and Legacy of Christopher Gadsden." Master's thesis, Clemson University, 2018.

Ferrari, Mary C. "Charity, Folly, and Politics: Charles Town's Social Clubs on the Eve of the Revolution." *South Carolina Historical Magazine* 112, nos. 1–2 (January–April 2011): 50–83.

Fraser, Walter J. *Patriots, Pistols, and Petticoats: Poor Sinful Charleston During the American Revolution.* University of South Carolina Press, 1993.

Frey, Sylvia. *Water from the Rock: Black Resistance in a Revolutionary Age.* Princeton University Press, 1991.

Garden, Alexander, Jr. (Major Garden). *Anecdotes of the American Revolution.* A.E. Miller, 1828.

———. *Anecdotes of the Revolutionary War in America*. A.E. Miller, 1822.

Godbold, Stanley, Jr., and Robert Woody. *Christopher Gadsden and the American Revolution.* University of Tennessee Press, 1983.

Gould, Christopher. "Robert Wells, Colonial Charleston Printer." *South Carolina Historical Magazine* 79, no.1 (January 1978): 23–49.

———. "Scottish Printers and Booksellers in Colonial Charleston, S.C." *Studies in Scottish Literature* 15, no. 1 (1980).

Harris, J. William. *The Hanging of Thomas Jeremiah: A Free Black Man's Encounter with Liberty.* Yale University Press, 2009.

Kaplan, Sidney, and Emma N. Kaplan. *The Black Presence in an Age of Revolution.* Belknap Press, 1989.

Kelly, Joseph. *America's Longest Siege: Charleston, Slavery, and the Slow March Toward Civil War*. Overlook Press, 2013.

Kelly, Joseph P. "Henry Laurens: The Southern Man of Conscience in History." *South Carolina Historical Magazine* 102, no. 2 (April 2006): 82–123.

Krawczynski, Keith. *William Henry Drayton: South Carolina Revolutionary Patriot.* Louisiana State University Press, 2001.

Lambert, Robert S. *South Carolina Loyalists in the American Revolution*. University of South Carolina Press, 1987.

Lumpkin, Henry. *From Savannah to Yorktown: The American Revolution in the South*. University of South Carolina Press, 1981.

Maier, Pauline. "The Charleston Mob and the Evolution of Popular Politics in Revolutionary South Carolina, 1765–1784." *Perspectives in American History* 4 (1970), 173–96.

Massey, Gregory. *John Laurens and the American Revolution.* University of South Carolina Press, 2000.

McCandless, Peter, *Slavery, Disease, and Suffering in the Southern Lowcountry.* Cambridge University Press, 2011.

McDonough, Daniel. *Christopher Gadsden and Henry Laurens: The Parallel Lives of Two American Patriots.* Susquehanna University Press, 2000.

Merrell, James. *The Indians' New World: Catawbas and Their Neighbors from European Contact Through the Era of Removal*. University of North Carolina Press, 1989.

National Gallery of Art. "Alexander Garden." History of Early American Landscape Design, https://heald.nga.gov.

Olwell, Robert A. "'Domestick Enemies': Slavery and Political Independence in South Carolina, May 1775–March 1776." *Journal of Southern History* 55, no. 1 (February 1989): 21–48.

———. *Masters, Slaves, & Subjects: The Culture of Power in the South Carolina Low Country, 1740–1790*. Cornell University Press, 1998.

Pancake, John. *This Destructive War: The British Campaign in the Carolinas, 1780–1782.* University of Alabama Press, 1985.

Piecuch, Jim. *Three Peoples, One King: Loyalists, Indians, and Slaves in the Revolutionary South, 1775–1782*. University of South Carolina Press, 2008.

Poston, Jonathan H. *The Buildings of Charleston: A Guide to the City's Architecture*. University of South Carolina Press, 1997.

Quarles, Benjamin. *The Negro in the American Revolution*. University of North Carolina Press, 1961.

Reid, Nina. "Loyalism and the Philosophic Spirit in the Scientific Correspondence of Dr. Alexander Garden." *South Carolina Historical Magazine* 92, no. 1 (January 1991): 5–14.

Rogers, George C. "The Charleston Tea Party: The Significance of December 3, 1773." *South Carolina Historical Magazine* 75, no. 3 (July 1974): 153–68.

Ryan, William R. *The World of Thomas Jeremiah: Charles Town on the Eve of the American Revolution*. Oxford University Press, 2010.

Schama, Simon. *Rough Crossings: Britain, the Slaves, and the American Revolution*. Vintage, 2009.

Shaffer, Arthur. *To Be an American: David Ramsay and the Making of the American Consciousness*. University of South Carolina Press, 1991.

Snap, J. Russell. *John Stuart and the Struggle for Empire on the Southern Frontier*. Louisiana University Press, 1996.

———. "William Henry Drayton: 'The Making of a Conservative Revolutionary.'" *Journal of Southern History* 57, no. 4 (November 1991): 637–58.

Thomas, Isaiah. *History of Printing in America*. J. Munsell, printer, 1874.

Uglow, Jenny. *The Lunar Men: Five Friends Whose Curiosity Changed the World*. Farrar, Strauss and Giroux, 2002.

Wade, N.J. *Destined for Distinguished Oblivion: The Scientific Vision of William Charles Wells*. Springer, 2003.

Wallace, David D. *The Life of Henry Laurens, with a Sketch of the life of Lieutenant-Colonel John Laurens*. G.P. Putnam's Sons, 1915.

Walsh, Richard. Charleston's Sons of Liberty: A Study of the Artisans, 1763–1789. University of South Carolina Press, 1959.

Waring, Joseph I. *History of Medicine in South Carolina*, vol. 1. *1660–1825*. South Carolina Medical Association, 1964.

Weir, Robert M. *The Last of American Freemen: Studies in the Political Culture of the Colonial and Revolutionary South*. Mercer University Press, 1986.

Wickwire, Franklin, and Mary Wickwire. *Cornwallis: The American Adventure*. Houghton Mifflin, 1970.

Wilson, David K. *The Southern Strategy: Britain's Conquest of South Carolina and Georgia, 1775–1780*. University of South Carolina Press, 2005.

Wood, Peter H. *Black Majority: Negroes in South Carolina from 1670 to the Stono Rebellion.* Alfred A. Knopf, 1974.

# INDEX

## H



## I



## J



## K



## L



## M

# T



# V



# W

## Y

# ABOUT THE AUTHOR

Peter McCandless received his PhD from the University of Wisconsin–Madison. He taught history at the College of Charleston, retiring as Distinguished Professor Emeritus. He won the college's Distinguished Teaching Award and was selected as a South Carolina Governor's Distinguished Professor. He has published many historical works, primarily on the history of medicine and disease in Britain and the United States. Much of his early work focused on mental disease, culminating in *Moonlight, Magnolias, and Madness: Insanity in South Carolina from the Colonial Period to the Progressive Era* (University of North Carolina Press, 1996). His book *Slavery, Disease, and Suffering in the Southern Lowcountry* (Cambridge University Press, 2011) was awarded the SHEAR Prize in 2012. He was an associate editor and contributor to *The South Carolina Encyclopedia* (2006). He loves tennis, birds, nature, art, sport and, of course, research and writing. He currently lives in London with his wife, Nalan.